The Unmapped Road
to
Happily Ever After

by

Shirley Shannon Coops

Dedicated to my brave ancestors.

Thanks to all the people I've known, including
the Santa Rosa Junior College life story writing class,
and teacher Suzanne Sherman.

Thank you to my Kenwood friend, Judy Watten,
who told me about the class and then cheered me on.

Thank you to my children, who encouraged me.

A special memory of my husband, Arthur Coops,
for his patience and support with my project.

TABLE OF CONTENTS

PART ONE: MY LIFE AS SHIRLEY SHANNON

PART TWO: ARTHUR IRVING COOPS AND SHIRLEY SHANNON COOPS

PART THREE: A GOOD MOVE AFTER ALL

ACKNOWLEDGEMENTS: GETTING IT TOGETHER

This story started before I was born. As I looked back at the decades, it seemed a good idea to record the history as it appeared to me. An opportunity presented itself when friend Judy Watten suggested I go to a life story writing class with her. It was through Santa Rosa Junior College with Suzanne Sherman teaching, and was held at Oakmont Gardens every Thursday afternoon. Surprisingly, there was no charge to participants.

Suzanne Sherman

On September 9, 2008, the adventure began. Soon after I started writing, I thought, *What if my computer loses these?* I was concerned, because my stories weren't backed up. Classmate Millie McKay said her friend and neighbor, Michael Martin, would help, and he did. Martin put my stories on a memory stick and a CD. He gave me computer advice and said he thought I could benefit from a computer class. There appeared to be consensus on that point. Diana Booker-Spry, a computer tutor, has been helping me map the mysterious land now at my fingertips.

Suzanne gave us a list of books that would be helpful in writing and organizing. I started with "Woe is I, The Grammarphobe's Guide to Better English," by Patricia T. O'Conner. "The Autobiographer's Handbook," edited by Jennifer Traig, presented advice by a "brain trust" of published authors who gave advice on getting started, finishing, and handling everything between, and how to cope once that's done.

I'd like to read some of the memoirs that are listed in the book. There's a category for "normal lives," which seems to fit me more than any of the more unusual examples, such as transformation, addiction, foods, and losses, although I suppose all lives have periods like that.

Suzanne said that Joyce Harr, a member of one of her other classes, was very good at organizing material into a finished product. Joyce agreed to come for a consultation. I was comforted by the fact that she's a grandma who had worked with computers from their beginning. She showed me examples of her work, including one by classmate, Caroline Ramberg. Joyce showed me several bindings, including "comb bound." She gave me some suggestions on how to proceed. We've been working together ever since.

Friend, neighbor, and classmate Judy said that the Library of Congress doesn't like spiral bindings because they don't stand up straight. It had never occurred to me to try to please the Library of Congress. But it wouldn't be good to have my book flip-flopping on our children's shelves either, if that's where they decided to put it. I decided on a paperback book style, and to have photos inserted in the texts of the stories. I went

Classmates: Ann Berger, Millie McKay, Judy Watten

through albums, boxes, and wall displays, and tried to choose pictures that portrayed the times. I also have my Grandma Shannon's album, which has pictures from the late 1800s and early 1900s, but it would probably be best to put them in a separate archive.

As my book neared completion, I had many questions about editing and proofreading. Talented friends came to the rescue: Lauren Ayers, Charlene Tomason, Anne Coffelt, and her mother Beth helped me. Also classmates Judy Watten and Millie McKay were always there to share their experience and give encouragement. My sincere thanks go to all these generous people.

◀◀ | ▶▶

QUESTIONS

Are there questions you wished you had asked your grandparents? I decided to give our grandchildren an opportunity to ask questions before completing my book, although there are difficulties with that because they don't yet know what they don't know. However, they did come up with quite a few inquiries. A couple of them asked about the Great Depression, and what it was like for me. How was I impacted? Where did I grow up, and how have things changed around there?

What about my school, the studies there, and my friends? Did I have the same friends all through school? How different was it then from how it is now? How are schools different? Did I have to take standardized tests? Conveniently, a grandchild had a school assignment in which she was assigned to ask a grandparent these questions. Other inquiries included: What age was my favorite, and why? What are some favorite memories? What did grandpa do in his job as an electrical engineer? The nine-year-old wondered if I'd seen my first airplane on TV.

Who was my favorite president during my lifetime, and why? An older grandson knew that I had mentioned Eisenhower. I had been thinking about Eisenhower's leadership abilities, the building of the Interstate Highway system, and the prosperity and low inflation, but I was asked if I remembered his warning about the military-industrial complex. I don't remember what I thought about it at the time, but have often heard it quoted. Since the 1950s other organizations have grown powerful and there are other "complexes." Corporations, labor unions, trial lawyers, conservation groups, and many other interest groups have potent political power.

How different was it then from how it is now? As I organized my book I answered questions from my perspective, and I acknowledge that not everyone would agree. I hope the stories themselves show how times have changed. I hope the nine-year-old grandson will understand that I saw my first airplane in the sky as soon as I could see and recognize anything. It was a couple of decades later before I first saw TV. I should mention that during my lifetime our country made the significant transition from largely agricultural to industrial.

It was hard to answer, "What was my favorite age, and why?" Each decade had its good times and its challenges. Parts of every age were my "favorite" as well as having "unfavorable" times, too. One unfavorable time was in 2003, when I discovered an incident that made the definition of "cheating" a question.

WWII was a principal defining event of a generation. Both the Depression and WWII seemed to have had equally important effects on me. They both helped to form most of my attitudes for the succeeding years. I don't think I can claim full membership in the "Greatest Generation" who won the war. Maybe I'm of the Norman Rockwell generation with an idealized picture of beautiful America.

Later generations' memories may have been etched by Vietnam or the Civil Rights movement, or maybe the terrorist attacks on September 11, 2001. Perhaps today the Big Recession will be remembered as influencing the course of their lives. They will be affected by spending patterns. More money going out than coming in has major effects on individuals, families, and governments.

Writing this book has been a wondrous journey back through the decades. I hope others will enjoy the trip with me.

PART ONE:

MY LIFE AS
SHIRLEY SHANNON

MATERNAL FAMILY TREE

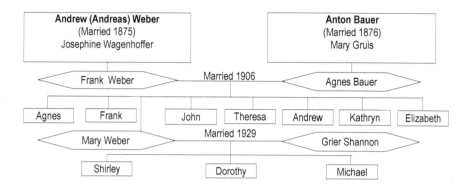

Andrew (Andreas) Weber	Anton Bauer
(Married 1875)	(Married 1876)
Josephine Wagenhoffer	Mary Gruis

Frank Weber — Married 1906 — Agnes Bauer

Agnes	Frank	John	Theresa	Andrew	Kathryn	Elizabeth

Mary Weber — Married 1929 — Grier Shannon

Shirley	Dorothy	Michael

PATERNAL FAMILY TREE

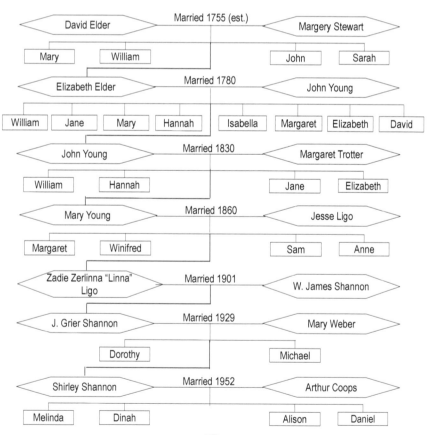

David Elder — Married 1755 (est.) — Margery Stewart

Mary	William	John	Sarah

Elizabeth Elder — Married 1780 — John Young

William	Jane	Mary	Hannah	Isabella	Margaret	Elizabeth	David

John Young — Married 1830 — Margaret Trotter

William	Hannah	Jane	Elizabeth

Mary Young — Married 1860 — Jesse Ligo

Margaret	Winifred	Sam	Anne

Zadie Zerlinna "Linna" Ligo — Married 1901 — W. James Shannon

J. Grier Shannon — Married 1929 — Mary Weber

Dorothy	Michael

Shirley Shannon — Married 1952 — Arthur Coops

Melinda	Dinah	Alison	Daniel

WE STAND ON THE SHOULDERS
OF MANY

How did I get to the point that I wanted to write about my life? When my husband was transferred to Pittsburgh in 1983, we had the first child-free home in nearly thirty years. It seemed like an opportunity to complete my documents for joining the DAR, and of course that takes considerable ancestor research.

The next step in genealogical study didn't start until the Internet became part of our lives. I began an e-mail correspondence with two cousins, and we shared memories and whatever material we already had. But real progress came with a cousin-in-law's desire to organize her husband's family background. She was quite thorough, and e-mails were flying in every direction. We tried to weave together scattered stories with genuine court records, although we found that official records weren't always accurate.

Frank Weber

It should have been easy to learn the nationality of my maternal grandparents, but even that took library research and further inquiry. A great-aunt, Mary Franz, said they were Austrian, not Hungarian. Ancestors moved from Austria to Hungary during the reign of Maria Theresa, Queen of Hungary (1740-1780), a woman also referred to as Kaiserina of Austria, Hungary, and Bohemia, now Czechoslovakia.

My grandparents were from this area. At the time of their birth, warfare caused constantly changing border lines. It was a puzzle to know which country ruled at a particular time. In school, they studied from

German schoolbooks until those were taken away and replaced with Hungarian books.

Records show that my grandfather, Franz (Frank) Weber was born in Wesnerm, Hungary, near Budapest, in 1880. He was the son of Andreas (Andrew) Weber and Josephine Wagenhoffer. He was one of the four surviving children from fourteen births.

In 1898, at age 18, he sailed from Antwerp, Belgium, on the ship Berlin, and arrived at Ellis Island. He was "in good health and had no prison record," and he had $5 in his pocket. He was to join his aunt and uncle, Franz Joseph, in S. Bethlehem, Pennsylvania.

The only other person I knew from that generation was "Rich Uncle Louis" Waggenhoffer, my grandfather's uncle. He arrived in New York in 1891, and settled in Idaho. He always gave us kids silver dollars when he came to visit.

Agnes Bauer Weber

My grandmother, Agnes Bauer, the daughter of Anton Bauer and Mary Gruis, was born in 1886 in Bakony Sharja, Hungary, also near Budapest. Anton's first wife was Mary's sister, so the thirteen children, two of which were twins, may have come from two different mothers. Eight children died at ages ranging from a few days to 15 years.

Mary was only 14 when she and Anton were married. My grandmother was one of the five surviving children. In 1902 at age 16 she emigrated aboard the ship Finland that departed from Antwerp, Belgium, bound for Ellis Island. The passenger record lists Jako, Hungary, as her place of residence at the time of emigration.

I don't know if Frank and Agnes knew each other in Europe, or didn't meet until later. In any case, dark-haired and dark-eyed Frank and blonde and blue-eyed Agnes were married in 1906 at St. Joseph Roman Catholic Church in Sharon, Pennsylvania. They hoped for a better life than what their ancestors had faced in Europe where they lived in political strife and poverty. Obviously, uncontrolled fertility was another problem. Living conditions were much better in this country, but birth control still was not acceptable even if it had been readily available. Frank and Agnes had eight children, the third of whom was my mother, Mary.

My paternal grandparents' stories are quite different. The first records I have say that the ancestral seat of the Elders was Elderslie, County of Renfrew, near Paisley, Scotland. They had a "coat of arms." Some of them came directly to America, while others first emigrated to northern Ireland. The Irish emigrants are among my ancestors.

In 1754 David Elder emigrated from Louch Island of Inch, or Lough Swilly, County Donegal, Ireland. His wife Margery, or Margaret, Stewart is said to have been a nobleman's daughter, highly educated, and very skillful in fancy needle work. David Elder's children claimed to be cousins of Sir Walter Scott.

My grandmother is descended from David and Margaret's daughter, Elizabeth. Elizabeth married John Young. Their son John was a private in Capt. Abraham Smith's company, Col. William Irvine's regiment, 6th battalion, Pennsylvania Infantry, Revolutionary War, enlisted Feb. 4, 1776. (Elizabeth's sister, Mary, was an ancestor of William and Alex McGuffey, authors of the McGuffey Readers and the McGuffey Spelling Books.)

Elizabeth and John Young's son, also named John, married Margaret Trotter. They had five children, one of which was Mary, my great-grandmother. She married Jesse Ligo, and they had four daughters and one son. Their oldest daughter, Zadie Zerlinna, is my grandmother.

II

As I read excerpts from family history, it's like getting thumbnail sketches of the birth and growth of our country. After the Revolutionary War, my ancestors on my father's side, which included the war veteran John Young and his wife Elizabeth Elder Young and their family, moved from Cumberland County in central Pennsylvania to Mercer County in the western part of the state.

Records found at the Mercer County Historical Society in Mercer, Pennsylvania, state that this involved traveling "through almost pathless woods." They brought wagons containing all of their worldly possessions. John was able to afford to buy a large tract of land. After making a clearing in the woods, he built a log cabin. It appears that the Young family had been well off in Scotland, and was able to take some resources to Ireland and thence to America. One record said that they left Ireland because of Roman Catholic persecution.

In this country, their log cabin was built with the help of slaves inherited by John's wife. The practice of slavery was becoming more widely recognized as the abominable practice it is, and he freed his slaves, but not until a slave reached the age of twenty-seven. In those pioneer days, the forest was home to many animals, and also "dusky savages," as some of the settlers called the American Indians.

John Young, Jr., born in 1797, was one of five surviving children of the nine that were born to John and Elizabeth. The record says that in school he was an "intelligent reader," and became well informed on the topics of the day. His father gave him 150 acres of the parental homestead in Wilmington Township, Mercer County, Pennsylvania, and he farmed it successfully. He married Margaret Trotter, and together they raised four children.

John and Margaret were brought up in the Presbyterian faith, and were liberal in their religious beliefs. They built a church on the home farm, and it was open for all denominations. John was an ardent abolitionist, and his house was one of the stations on the underground railway in Mercer County. One of the sons, William, fought in the Civil War. William was "an earnest supporter of the principles of the Republican party." This quote is also from a paper at the Historical Society.

William's sister, Mary, is my great-grandmother. She married Jesse Ligo in 1860. My grandmother is one of the five children born to this union. The family name, Ligo, has an interesting history, according to the Dictionary of Family Names of the United Kingdom by Mark Antony Lower. It states that Ligo is a contraction of Linlithgow to Lithgow to Ligo. Lithgow is a well-known Scottish town.

Jesse Ligo's parents, Samuel and Mary Johnston Ligo, came from Derbyshire, England. Samuel was naturalized in 1836. I have a copy of the land purchase that Samuel made in 1830. He paid $1450 for 150 acres of land. It appears that Samuel prospered. His will, dated 1876, is a work of art in itself with its wonderful old-fashioned handwriting. The will leaves generous bequests to his children. Mary's name isn't on either the land purchase or the will. There is evidence that it was often the custom for men to have their names on deeds, etc., excluding their wives. Male heirs inherited estates, with widows and daughters being dependent on their generosity. This was likely the case with Mary Ligo. Mary didn't die young. The record said she died in 1872 at age 70.

Samuel and Mary's son, Jesse Ligo, is my great-grandfather. He along with his brother John were executors of their father's will. They received bequests of land, stocks, and bonds. Another brother, Luther, wasn't included in the will, but it's possible he received his share early to fill a special need. Or was he out of favor with his father? We don't know.

Fraternal Grandparents, Aunts, and Uncles
Standing: Grandmother Linna Ligo Shannon, her sister-in-law Frances Garrett Ligo, unmarried sister Winifred Ligo, sister Margaret Ligo Clark, sister Anne Ligo Edeburn.
Kneeling: Grandfather W. James Shannon, Grandma's brother Samuel Ligo, brothers-in-law Harry Clark and Hiram Edeburn.

A granddaughter, Elizabeth, received Samuel's black mare, buggy and harness. Samuel and Mary Johnston Ligo are the beginning of the annual July 4 Ligo family reunions, the first of which was July 4, 1917. They are still being held, as of 2010.

Four of the five children of great-grandparents Jesse Ligo and Mary Young had ordinary names. However, my grandmother was named Zadie Zerlinna. I haven't been able to find any explanation except that her mother had been reading a novel with a character by that name.

Zadie Zerlinna (Linna) Ligo and W. James (Jim) Shannon were married in 1901. Linna was 40 and Jim was 45. My father, born in 1903, was an only child. Linna's sister Margaret had only one child, and her brother, Samuel, fathered two. Sister Anne didn't have children, and Winifred never married. This low birthrate arouses my curiosity. It's so different from my stories before this one.

Aunt Winnie supported herself as a seamstress at Dixmont Hospital near Pittsburgh. One of Aunt Winnie's jobs was to make the patients' gowns. When she retired she lived with her sisters' families. One sister was Anne Edeburn who was married to Hiram (Hite) Edeburn. They lived in Butler, Pennsylvania, about 30 miles from our house. Aunt Winnie, Aunt Annie and Uncle Hite were important people in my young life, as were Harry Clark, a deceased sister's husband, and their daughter, Mary. Harry and Mary lived in Grove City, a college town about 18 miles from our house.

Uncle Sam Ligo lived on a farm near Mercer with his son and daughter-in-law, Russell and Esther. I played with my cousins; Bernice, Billy and Dickie. A descendant, Jesse Ligo, Jr., still lives on that farm.

W. (William) J. Shannon, 1890

It was a special time when we went to visit these folks. Sometimes we went for Thanksgiving. Occasionally when I was walking home from school I could see Aunt Annie's and Uncle Hite's car at our house. I knew who it was because they were the only ones who parked up beside our back porch.

I don't have much information on the Shannons. Great-grandfather John Shannon was born in Ireland in 1830. He arrived in Philadelphia, Pennsylvania, and traveled from there to Racine, Wisconsin. He was granted citizenship in 1856. He married Sarah Taylor, who was also from Ireland. My grandfather, Jim Shannon, was born in Wisconsin. At some point they moved to western Pennsylvania.

A family story is that Jim really loved trains and the romance of the rail. An industry that was to become a powerful force in the American story was just getting started. Jim found a railroad job that he truly enjoyed. But word came from home that his father needed him on the farm. So at age 23 he dutifully left his job and went home to help. It's unfortunate that duty called, because farming wasn't his calling. But his family was his first concern. The record says that he was successful and was held in high esteem by many friends.

It would be interesting to know how Linna and Jim met and married. Linna was 42 when my father, J.(esse) Grier, was born in 1903. As far as I know, he didn't use his first name, Jesse.

LET ME CALL YOU SWEETHEART

It's difficult to picture the environment in which my mother grew up. My father's is easier, because I grew up in the same place that he did. But my mother's parents were recent immigrants. They settled in Farrell, Pennsylvania, a town in the western part of the state. My grandfather worked in a steel mill.

My maternal grandparents, Frank and Agnes Bauer Weber, had eight children in fifteen years. Baby girl Agnes and baby boy Frank were the first two, and then my mother, Mary, arrived next, and the other five came in regular succession. Blondes and brunettes, brown-eyed and blue-eyed, in pictures it's clear they were pretty children.

The house must have got noisier as it became more crowded every year. My mother said that sometimes her mother had to just go outside and walk around the block. That is easy to believe. Although she was basically a sweet-tempered woman, it had to be a difficult life. Her husband was a tough German father. He was quite strict with the children, and didn't spare the rod. But he provided for their needs.

Agnes Bauer Weber & Frank Weber with their first three children: my mother, Mary, with Agnes, and Frank.

All eight children survived, and Grandma Weber credited her old German medical book with helping her tend to their illnesses. My mother survived both diphtheria and rheumatic fever. Grandma's good nourishing food helped, too. She fixed wonderful soups and stews which were often enhanced with plump dumplings or homemade noodles.

Only the German language had been spoken until the older children went to school and learned English. The children did well in school. It's unfortunate that they were forced to quit before graduating. Their father demanded that they go to work to help support the family. Agnes, the oldest child, started ninth grade, but her father came and got her and said she had to get a job. She was 14. Her small wages as a housekeeper were all given to her father. Gradually she was able to keep 1/4 of her pay, and at age 18 she was allowed half.

My mother was also first a household helper. Her employer was a prosperous lawyer. This did serve to further her education as she saw life from a different perspective. She often talked about her good experiences with the family. Grandmother Weber convinced her husband that half the wages would be enough to take.

My mother's next job was with Westinghouse Electric's Transformer Division in the adjoining city of Sharon.

Mother, Mary Weber, 1926

She worked there for five years and managed to save quite a bit of money. This was commendable because she had only half her wages for herself.

Meanwhile, back on a 170-acre farm in a nearby area of Mercer County, Pennsylvania, my father was growing up in very different circumstances. His mother was 42 and his father 47 when he was born, and he was the only one they had. It must have been a silent world compared to my mother's home. There were numerous relatives who occasionally came to visit. My great-grandmother lived there for a while. Care in old age was the family's responsibility.

My father worked on the farm with his father as they tended animals and grew crops. I'm not sure what the main output was. At one time or another they had milk cows, pigs, chickens, and sheep. Work horses did the heavy lifting. Possible crops were corn, oats, and wheat. Every

21

Father, Grier Shannon, 1921

summer they put up hay.

My father always enjoyed sports, with baseball being his favorite. He played softball as long as he was able. Pitching horseshoes was another past time. He liked basketball, too, and, in high school he was on the team. At some point after high school, he went to mechanics' school in Detroit. I don't know the circumstances of his going there, but he did become an expert machinist. It's sad to think that both my father and grandfather were farming when their principal talents were in other occupations. My father liked machines and my grandfather liked railroads. It appears that family duty kept them in place.

Music and dancing were popular, and therein lies the beginning of another story. My father and mother both liked to dance. My father and some friends had access to cars and would drive to the larger town of

May 1, 1927

Parents: Mary Weber and Grier Shannon

Sharon to check out the scenes there. Sometimes they would go to dances that were held at the Buhl (named for a local industry leader) Girls Club.

On one particular evening both Mary Weber and Grier Shannon were there. They were immediately attracted to each other. By the end of the evening when the band played Let Me Call You Sweetheart, Grier asked, "Can I call you sweetheart?" and Mary said, "Yes." This was about 1925 when my mother was 17 and my father 22. For the next four years his car knew the way to Farrell. My mother was so happy. Besides thinking he was really nice, she had been determined to marry a real "American," and he was certainly that.

She was often at the farm and had to have noticed that the farm had none of the modern conveniences that she took for granted. But love conquered all and these two very different backgrounds were merged in 1929. This could have been the beginning of a fairy tale marriage, but it was 1929 and the financial world was about to collapse.

THE MORNING AFTER

It was a lovely little wedding on April 2, 1929. Officiating at the ceremony uniting my Roman Catholic mother and Protestant father was the Rev. Leslie Mountford, a Presbyterian pastor. My mother came to believe that this was the first of too many concessions. But at the time it didn't bother her very much. She had the man she wanted and she was ready to get married and have a family of her own.

My Parents' Wedding Day: April 2, 1929

My mother had moved her belongings into her fiancée's family home on the outskirts of Mercer, Pennsylvania, and that's where they went after the ceremony. A couple of things then happened that didn't portend an easy future. First, when my grandmother said that she was so happy because she had always wanted a daughter, my mother replied, "I already have a mother."

Then the new bride was upset when early the next morning her mother-in-law called up the stairs, "Hey, Grier, time to get up." The cows had to be milked and the other chores done before breakfast. Somehow adjustments and accommodations must have been made, because my mother was soon pregnant. It wasn't in the first month of her marriage as she had hoped, but in the second month when I was on the way.

The delivery must have been very difficult and painful. It was at home with no anesthetic. But a doctor did come to the house when I was born on March 13, 1930. They said they had hoped for a girl and I always believed them. No doubt I received lots of attention, because I was the first grandchild on both sides of the family. I was taken on visits and people came to the house to see the baby. My first big event may have

24

been the Ligo family reunion that was held every July 4. I have a picture of me at three months, the youngest, being held by the oldest person, ninety-three-year-old Mary Ligo.

I had the attention of my parents and grandparents all the time since they all lived there. My Grandfather Shannon died when I was only three. I have a copy of his obituary. He was a "highly respected resident of East Lackawannock Township." My uncle had a copy among his records, and he added his own comment that he liked my grandfather. He had never heard him say a cross word to anyone. He was kind and good to everybody, and he loved his family, especially his granddaughter (me).

Ligo Reunion July 4, 1930: 93-year-old Mary Ligo holding Shirley

It's hard to speculate exactly how my mother had foreseen married life, but it wasn't long before she didn't at all like the way things were going. In better economic times it might have been possible for them to soon have a little house of their own. She was miserable living in somebody else's house. That was worse than the house not having electricity or running water. She told me that sometimes she would carry me out to the woods, sit on a stump, hold me, and cry.

These were all good people. My sister and I often talk about how the situation might have been improved. We grew up with the constant refrain, "I want my own home." That didn't happen for a long time because my grandmother lived to be ninety-seven. She was a dear, sweet woman that everybody liked. It's just that the house was really hers, although she would have lost it without my parents paying the bills. Grandma had no income and was totally dependent.

As I look back on the situation it does appear that my father should have taken some kind of action. He seemed to believe that nothing could be changed. It's true there was no money. He struggled to keep up payments on a loan that we would now consider negligible. Everybody worked so hard. Cooking and baking were done on a wood stove. A garden was tended in the summer, and the produce had to be preserved with arduous bouts of canning. Pigs were butchered and chickens beheaded to provide main courses. There was churning to be done for our butter, and fruit to be made into juice, jams, and jellies.

Mother, Mary Weber Shannon, and Shirley

Their lives must have been very hard, but for small me everything was just dandy. I had plenty to eat and nice clothes to wear. My mother was a talented seamstress. I also received pretty clothes from a family friend who wasn't suffering as much economically. When my mother bought new shoes for me, it was always a happy day. Before going to bed, I would put the shoes on top of a chest of drawers so I'd be able to see them first thing in the morning.

Uncle Andy bicycled the sixteen miles from Farrell to come visit, and always brought candy. He taught me my ABCs. He had good games including one with the globe. We would try to stump each other about where in the world a place was. He also convinced me that he had absolutely seen the Easter bunny's tracks outside. Uncle Andy and my father got along well. They joked around and called each other Hank and Cy.

I don't remember feeling lonesome or bored. I had an active imagination and was able to invent games and entertain myself. There weren't children around, but there was always somebody. I saw other children at church. Sunday School was okay, but in the sanctuary children were to be seen and not heard. If I made any noise my father took me to the car and I was spanked. In Sunday School Mrs. Taylor told us many interesting things such as Methuselah being very, very, very, old. I know I learned more than that. But the most important part to me was being with other children.

◄◄ | ►►

JOYS AND CONCERNS OF LIVING IN THE 1930s

We hardly had any money. The family's income was from selling milk and some butter and eggs. Some families couldn't manage and went on relief, which is what welfare was called then. But there was a severe stigma on those who did. Doing such a thing never crossed my folks' minds. Since I'd never known anything different than the way things were I didn't recognize any problem.

I soon learned that a person named Roosevelt was important. He had said something about "there's nothing to fear but fear itself." My father's response was, "That's what he thinks." My mother's fervent wish for her own home appeared to be unattainable. There was no money for another house, and my father's parents needed his care and support.

There were fun things, too, amidst my mother's constant complaining. I often got to ride along in the car when my mother or father went on errands. One day my father and I were coming in our driveway and chickens were running back and forth across the road as chickens do. My father blew the horn to get them out of the way. Evidently this triggered one of my very first sentences "Bad daddy blow horn scare chookies." He laughed so hard and he must have repeated it several times. I wouldn't remember it otherwise.

Friends and neighbors had something called the Linger Longer Club. They met at each others' houses. The carpets were rolled up, the Victrola played, and the folks danced. There were grange meetings, too, with occasional parties and square dancing. The fiddler, the caller, and the whirling couples were fun to watch.

Meanwhile, this Mr. Roosevelt was starting many new projects. One was called the W.P.A. It touched our lives when a gang of men carrying sledgehammers walked behind a truck that dumped rocks all over the road. The men broke the rocks into smaller pieces, which were then covered with dirt. Our dirt road became passable in rainy weather.

Another huge improvement was the Rural Electrification Act. We eagerly watched the poles being placed and finally reaching our house. My mother was thrilled to get rid of the old oil lamps with their constant maintenance and inadequate light. She was sick of washing the chimneys, filling the lamps with oil, and trimming wicks. She threw out every lamp. I wish she had put some in the attic.

My life was fine and became even more interesting when a baby sister arrived in 1935 when I was five and a half. She was born at home so I got to see her very soon. I was fascinated with this tiny baby lying crossways on the seat of a rocking chair. She was named Dorothy Edith.

Shirley and sister Dorothy, 1936

Aunts and uncles came and fussed over us.

When my sister was one year old I was old enough to start first grade. I'd never been with so many children at one time before and it was scary and exciting. It wasn't easy to get to school. The two high school students who lived nearby had to walk the whole three miles to Mercer.

I walked about 1/4 mile. I started on the level and then went down a long hill to catch the bus, which was a neighbor's car with a school bus sign on the roof. Sometimes it was really cold when I walked. I remember one morning the snow had such a hard crust that it would bear my weight. I was crawling on my hands and knees while pushing my lunch box ahead of me. I had progressed only a few feet away from the back porch when my father saw what was happening. He said I really didn't have to go to school that day.

My first and second grades were in the same room. My teacher was Miss Achsah (a name from the book of Joshua in the Bible) Wallace. Miss Wallace hurried us into cursive writing. For some reason she didn't really approve of printing and that's been a handicap for me. There were two other rooms and teachers for first and second grades. One room was for all first grade and the other for all second grade. These were unofficially

28

known as the dumb rooms.

I have mostly good memories from those early grades. Miss Wallace did get impatient with me when I often forgot to dot the "i" in Shirley. But I never felt the sting of any of the paddles in her collection. She would bring the paddles out occasionally and slap them one by one against her leg. Children got the idea of how that would feel against their backsides. I don't remember that discipline was a big problem for me. I was very quiet and not inclined to plot mischief. I was still learning to get along with other children, while also getting started with reading and writing. These new and exciting experiences required all my attention.

One of the nicest things that happened was that I immediately found a best friend, Nina Ruth Smith. After 70 years we still correspond. We spent many happy hours together at school, at each other's homes, riding our bikes, talking on the phone (when we finally got one), writing letters, and in school activities. Nina's father was a mailman in Mercer.

Another good friend was also a mailman's daughter. Her father was our rural carrier. My father was his substitute carrier. They used their own cars to drive from mailbox to mailbox. Freda Zahniser and I liked to spend time

Shirley and sister Dorothy, 1937

at each other's homes. Freda's parents took in tourists and sometimes customers would stop and ask for a room. Then we had to sleep in a room over the garage. Both Nina's and Freda's homes had distinctive smells. The odors weren't unpleasant. I would recognize them now if the smells could be reproduced. That would bring back happy memories.

All the parents showed enormous patience. Once Freda and I were making caramel candy. Her mother's cooking pan was unusual. It had a

29

detachable handle, which detached as the boiling pot was being moved from stove to counter. The caramel candy spilled on the kitchen floor and quickly hardened there.

One of the unfortunate things that happened in first grade was that I caught several communicable diseases and took them home to my baby sister. She could have died from the measles. I also shared chicken pox and whooping cough. My whooping cough didn't go away completely until spring.

After a few years my sister was able to play and we had some fun games around the farm. We climbed up on the chicken house roof and used chalk to mark off rooms for our playhouse. The roof slanted only slightly. It had a black surface on which the white chalk showed up very well. Another of our playhouses was in the pasture field where my father had piles of rocks and boulders that he had removed from his crop-producing fields. Imagination fashioned stones into chairs and other useful furniture.

In the barn we could climb up onto the beam and jump into the hay. Patient old work horses, Billy and Bess, provided rides either on their backs or pulling wagons. I was terrified the first time my father put me up on the horse's back. What a huge animal! But I soon came to love it and begged for "just a little ride."

I'll admit that sometimes I used the know-how of my superior age to get my way with Dorothy and be mean. When we were older, Dorothy told me she never understood why I hated our tan cotton stockings and the support harnesses. Why did we hide them in the coal house under the coal? She was younger and didn't mind the stockings. I hope she doesn't also remember when I tricked her into touching the electric fence. But she probably does.

We were both in on the bathtub caper. It was so exciting to get a bathroom with a real tub. We had always used a tin tub in the middle of the kitchen floor. So there was the new tub and running water to fill it, which we proceeded to do right away. After our long luxurious bath we let the water out. Unfortunately, the drain wasn't connected yet and the water ran into the cellar. Our parents, especially our father, weren't happy.

The toilet was a great joy. We didn't have to always use the chamber pot in the hall or the two-seater outhouse. Out there we used crumpled up-pages of Sears Roebuck and Montgomery Ward catalogs for toilet paper.

Gradually we acquired some modern conveniences. My mother thought it was none too soon since she had always taken electricity and running water for granted in town.

◀ | ▶

THE 1930S WEREN'T ALL BAD

Our 170-acre farm in Mercer County, Pennsylvania had a pretty setting. Down the road in both directions the land was flat for a while, but then it was all downhill. We had a choice of three hills to get to the main road. All the hills were slippery in the winter and sometimes, after getting stuck on one hill, we would go try another one. Ours was the original road, but when the new one was built it had been constructed around our hill.

In nice weather we could walk to interesting spots around the farm. The three bubbling springs were some of my favorite places. The spring in the pasture field provided a steady source of fresh water for the animals. Another spring was on the edge of some woods. It was a shady and mossy site that inspired imagination. The third spring was in yet another direction. Perhaps somebody once lived near there and planted the daffodils that still bloomed every year. Walks around the farm lasted long enough that we would need a bathroom, which we found wherever we happened to be. Once I wiped with the aptly named smart weed.

We didn't have a spring or spring house at our house and I was sorry about that. I envied our neighbors who had those cool pleasant places where they could keep butter and milk. We did have a milk house with permanently installed water tubs. The various processes of milk product preparation were done here. The well provided plenty of water but it did require energetic pumping for the water to flow.

Our chickens enjoyed an idyllic life, except for the ones that became dinner. Each mother hen had her own little house. Every year there were about six individual chicken coops around our backyard. Each setting hen had her nest and her clutch of eggs to incubate. When the chicks hatched and were able to get around she would cluck as she led them to find things to eat. If she found something especially tasty she would make her "come for a treat" noise. Sometimes a chick would wander away from the others and then would make a pathetic "I'm lost" cheep. In the evening and at nap times we would see the mother take the chicks under her wings.

When we said we were going to town that meant Mercer, which was about three miles away. It was the county seat where a beautiful courthouse had been constructed. Mercer was the hub of several major state routes. My school, some stores, a library, churches, and a movie theater were there. Going to Sharon and Farrell, which were about 18 miles distant, was an adventure. There were streetcars and big stores. Most industry was located in this area. Traveling as far as Lake Erie 60 miles to the north seldom happened. Pittsburgh was 60 miles to the south and was a big city that I had never seen.

We went to church regularly. I don't remember how old I was when a lady convinced me to join the W.C.T.U. (Women's Christian Temperance Union). I don't think I ever did anything about it. Alcohol was never in our house so I didn't suffer the consequences of unwise drinking. My Grandfather Weber enjoyed a drink. During Prohibition he made his own blackberry wine.

My father was an expert mechanic and we always had a car in good repair. Since he worked on machines, he often questioned why our country didn't use the metric system.

Besides church, we went shopping, to the Grange for business meetings and social events, visited friends and relatives, attended 4-H meetings, and went to piano lessons. The library, which was upstairs from a business office, was a regular stop. Miss Kim, the librarian, was always helpful. In winter the library was heated with some sort of oil heater. Wet wool clothes in that heat took on a distinctive odor, which I liked. My sister and I played library at home with our books. We made check-out cards and pockets to hold them in the backs of the books.

Going to the movies was a special treat. What marvelous films were made in that decade! Have *The Wizard of Oz* and *Gone with the Wind* ever been surpassed? I knew who the movie stars were then. I had paper dolls of several of the famous ones. I liked radio, too, and didn't want to miss my favorite adventure stories, mysteries, romances, and music.

I wasn't named after Shirley Temple. I was four years old when she became famous. I joined many other little girls in having my hair tortured into a mass of curls. The Shirley Temple dolls were beautiful and I longed to have one of my own. I even entered a contest with a doll being the prize but I wasn't successful in ever getting one.

Mickey Mouse was a comic favorite. I wanted a Mickey Mouse watch just like Nina's. When Christmas came I excitedly opened a watch-size box. But my mother had decided to get me a "pretty" watch and not the ugly Mickey. I must have lamented that for years because my kids bought a Mickey Mouse watch for me. I don't remember if it was the wrist size or the big one that hangs on the wall. I have both.

When I was in about third grade we finally got a telephone. I was very glad because when my parents said a call had to be made it was my job to walk down the road and ask to use a neighbor's phone. My friend, Nina, already had a phone and we did love to talk. The operator would say, "Number, please." I would say "5-M, please." I think our number was 326-J-3. There was a 326-R-3, too, so altogether there were six parties on our line. We could hear three of the rings; one ring, two rings, or our three rings. Listening in was an interesting pastime.

At the 4-H meetings my mother was one of the leaders who taught us to cook and sew. The county home economist sometimes came to meetings. One year, when our project was home improvement, the economist expressed her interest in refinishing furniture. For some reason she was in our attic and saw an old desk-bookcase. She said, "Look at this curly maple trim!" This sparked my interest and I refinished a number of pieces over the years, long after 4-H days. The desk-bookcase is in my house now, as is a beautiful old storage piece. I also have a couple of chairs that I refinished and then wove new cane seats for them. One chair was originally a 4-H project.

I remember a number of 4-H sewing projects. (4-H stands for Head, Heart, Hands, Health.) We started out making aprons and gradually advanced to making dresses. I was never completely satisfied with a dress's fit. My most successful projects were years later when I made beautiful maternity clothes. Fit wasn't as much of a problem. Later, I liked sewing dresses for my own little girls.

I don't remember many cooking projects, but some clubs had more. Every year we went to a 4-H Roundup where finished projects were displayed and awarded ribbons. I remember I got a blue ribbon for my green checked dress. I received other awards but don't remember them specifically. There were beautiful baked goods and candy. Some clubs raised animals and others learned furniture making. There was a large variety of projects. 4-H also sponsored a camp, which I occasionally attended. The only criticism I have of 4-H is that parents could become too pushy. Some children received more than their fair share of help and attention. Perhaps this is a universal problem.

When I was little we had an interesting old pump organ. I don't know what happened to it. My maternal grandparents had a player piano that was great fun. All the grandchildren enjoyed it. Just put a roll in and start pumping and the piano did the rest. I agreed with my mother that it would be nice to learn to really play a piano. My parents sacrificed to provide lessons and I really did try. I practiced faithfully but for some reason was never able to make the piano part of my life. So many teachers did their best. Mrs. Armstrong was first. The main thing I remember about those lessons is that we got our beagle-spaniel pup from her cocker spaniel's litter. Mrs. Armstrong had all their tails cut off because she expected them to grow up to be cocker spaniels. But we had a beagle hound with no tail, which was unique. His name was Noisy.

Mrs. Mountford, our pastor's wife, was the next to try her hand with making me a pianist. She was a lovely lady. But my most vivid memory of going to her house for my lessons is that she complained about my fingernails clicking on the keys. One day she became exasperated and took me out on the back porch and cut my fingernails. To this day I like to keep my nails short.

In high school I was still trying to learn the piano. Miss Francis was the new band, orchestra, and

High School Graduation 1948
Mercer, PA

choir director. She was a lovely pianist and I longed to play as she did. I did my scales and continued to practice Chopin, Beethoven, Bach, church hymns, and popular sheet music.

Time passed and I graduated and went to work at Westinghouse. Now I paid for my own lessons and decided to ask Sister Marie Claire, a nun at St. Joseph Church, to give me lessons. She had a star pupil from Mercer who was a stunning success. Maybe there was hope for me. Not really. I was okay but not a natural. After eight years of lessons over a period of a dozen years I faced the fact that the piano had won.

My piano's troubles weren't over when I quit taking lessons. After I had my own house and had daughters I wanted them to have lessons. The older two think that was quite worthwhile. They say they can still read music, and say it helps with math skills, too. Our third daughter didn't have lessons, and regrets that she still can't read the bass clef.

Then we had a little boy, too. He had a pounding board with pegs that he could hammer down. He often did that, so when I heard pounding I thought nothing of it. Then I went to check on him and found that he had not been pounding his board. He had removed the little overhangs on most of the piano's ivories.

It was a disappointment to my mother that neither her children nor grandchildren ever learned to play the piano "by ear." That's probably a skill that a person either has or doesn't have. I think that Dorothy and I both feel that we didn't quite live up to expectations. We do have some skills but not exactly what our mother had in mind. I don't remember our grandmother criticizing us. It wasn't her nature to find fault or be unkind. But she did cry once when she saw us playing cards on Sunday.

As the 1930s moved on, my mother hadn't got any closer to having her own home. We often heard the Bible verse, "A man shall leave his mother and father and cleave unto his wife." We heard her talk about other women who took drastic steps to get their own homes. The most common tactic was to leave the husband and go back home. This wasn't an option for my mother. Her parents were gradually getting a smaller household as children married and left. They weren't going to take any of them back.

My mother's siblings came to visit us at the farm. Gradually new cousins came, too. I think my aunts and uncles liked the farm but sometimes they said mean things. They were a touchy bunch with easily bruised feelings. Sometimes they made "helpful" suggestions that were not appreciated. But they were unfailingly kind to the children.

I liked all my aunts and uncles. Uncle Andy called me Hedy Pepper. Aunt Betty said I should like that because there was a beautiful movie star named Hedy. Aunt Betty was beautiful. The Weber siblings stood out in a crowd. My uncles were about 6' tall and my mother and aunts about 5'8".

My father was an only child so there weren't as many visitors from his side. One of his aunts and her husband lived in Butler, which was about 30 miles away. From time to time my grandmother went to stay with them for a while. A maiden aunt also lived in that house.

Meanwhile, my mother continued to garden, can, cook and bake, all of which she did with great skill. She also had artistic talents that she expressed with sewing and other needle craft. She had high hopes for us and she did the best she knew how to help us.

GROWING UP WITH "COLORED PEOPLE"

Barack Obama's election made me think of my own experiences with the black community in the 1930s and 1940s. Colored folks, as they were called, seemed to fit right in at my school and neighborhood. But I'm sure they were suffering prejudices that I knew nothing about; one was my friend, Edna Phillips.

We often sat on the school bus together. Once we walked the three miles to Mercer to go to a movie. I remember a neighbor looked a little worried when she saw us together. But we got along fine.

Later when Edna got married I went to her wedding. The Phillips family lived a couple of miles away. Edna was married under a tree in the front yard. She moved away and I didn't see her for quite a while. When

Edna with her husband, Norman Brown, at her retirement from the Philadelphia Schools in 1997

I did see her one day I asked how she and her husband were, and she breezily replied, "Oh, I divorced him." I didn't see her again after that.

When I told my sister, Dorothy, that I was writing about Edna she said, "Didn't I tell you that she's back in the neighborhood? When she retired she came back and built a house on the family property." Then my sister told me the local paper had been running a series of stories about area families, and the Phillips family had just been featured. This was in 2008. Dorothy sent the article, and it told of the family with the sixteen children. There were several pictures of Edna. One picture was of Edna and her husband, Norman Brown.

This started a further investigation. Now that I knew her new family name I was able to get her address and phone number. I called her and we had a nice chat even though we hadn't seen each other for at least sixty years. She said that she had been so very glad to get out of Mercer, in western PA, and she went to Philadelphia, where she met her second husband. She hoped to become a nurse, and although that didn't happen, she did work in a VA hospital for many years. She and her husband moved back to the Mercer area, and she was just as glad to be back as she had been to leave. She loves being out of the city. Unfortunately, her husband of 49 years died in 2003, only two years after they built their new house. We were able to catch up on other family news. She's having some trouble remembering things, and is fearful that she will fall victim to Alzheimer's Disease as her father did.

My maternal grandparents lived in a mixed-race neighborhood in Farrell, PA, and being with black people was a normal part of life. I do remember that Farrell usually had a championship basketball team.

There were black businesses. One was a welding shop in Mercer where I occasionally went along when my father needed something welded that he couldn't do himself. They were simply part of the community. I'm not perceptive and I never sensed problems. I only found out about the troubles they had when I read about them later. The annual Westinghouse Minstrel Show, which featured white men in black face, must have been offensive to the black community. The minstrel show was sponsored by Westinghouse Electric Corp. where I worked.

While I was working there, a friend and I traveled through some of the southern states. I couldn't miss the "colored" signs on drinking fountains. Later when my husband and I traveled with our children, we had to stop at Laundromats occasionally. I noticed the "colored" and "white" signs and I started to divide our clothes into colored clothes and white clothes. My husband looked at me with some surprise and pointed out that, "They mean people." So my naivete continued.

I don't remember working with black people at Westinghouse. Perhaps it was against company policy to hire blacks in the office, although many blacks worked in the shop. I had few contacts with any people of color after my school days. I only watched as "Negroes" and "colored folks" started to be called "blacks, " "people of color," or the current "African-Americans."

I've never again felt the comfort that I felt with Edna and other colored families, and I'm not sure why. The fierce Civil Rights movement made me feel awkward and guilty, and as though I were one of the oppressors. But the black families changed, too. I'd known mother, father, and children in the "colored" community, which was no different than the white. But then more and more children were born to unwed mothers, and the collapse of black families has been devastating.

Now Barack Obama has been elected president of the United States. It's such an extraordinary and history-making event, and his election has inspired great hope. I try not to dwell on the racial aspects. Obama's mother was white. Would he have been elected if he had married a white woman and had white children? Race relations are complicated.

PUBERTY AND WWII,
EQUALLY TRAUMATIC

I had never before felt that everything was out of control. What was going on? My body was becoming unfamiliar to me. I suddenly put on weight and looked pudgy. My dear Aunt Hazel was on the heavy side, and she happily declared, "Oh, you're going to be just like me!" I loved Aunt Hazel but really didn't want to copy her figure. Then my mother told me I could expect to "come sick," as menstruating was sometimes called. What happened to my simple, uncomplicated life? It was never to return.

Exactly when did things start to change? Third and fourth grade had been all right. Fourth grade seemed so much more grown up than third. We had more books. I especially liked our big and impressive geography book. Miss Patterson was the third grade teacher. A classmate, Royce Waha, aroused her anger when he gave an impertinent answer when she asked for a sentence using the word "ever." He said, "Miss Patterson kisses Mr. Boles ever day." She slapped his face. Miss Patterson didn't marry Mr. Boles, but did marry Mr. Ringer. For fourth grade she came back as Mrs. Ringer. I should explain that first and second grades were together, as were third and fourth, and also fifth and sixth.

Fifth and sixth grades with Miss Nelson were okay for me, but my sister, Dorothy, had trouble there. For instance, when Dorothy got her literature book, she read the whole thing right away. Then she wasn't interested when Miss Nelson talked about a story that Dorothy had read several weeks before. Dorothy thought that Miss Nelson was mean and cruel. Miss Nelson thought that Dorothy and her friend, Evelyn, should be in Miss Knoll's sixth grade, informally known as Wiggy Knoll's dumb room. Dorothy later told me that she and Evelyn had decided to run away from home rather than be in what they believed was the sixth grade holding cell. However, they had no idea where to go.

My parents suffered a personal sadness in these years. My mother still didn't have her own home, and she blamed grandma for all misfortunes including the one when she lost her baby. She said she would never have been on that wagon when the horses ran away if she hadn't been trying to get out of the house for a while. The wagon being pulled by the spooked horses raced over the extremely rough road, and the severe shaking caused a miscarriage. This happened in the early 1940s.

The whole world was in the tumult of WWII as I was going through the awkward growing-up years. I know that many people were suffering horribly, and now it seems silly to talk about my normal little problems. My first dates were with a neighbor boy. We often walked the three miles into Mercer to see a movie and then drink a Coke. It was all rather strange because we were both very quiet people.

Schoolwork wasn't a problem. I also worked on the school paper and the yearbook, and was in plays and music programs. I tried to play the saxophone, which I did on about the same amateur level as piano. A wonderful older couple, Frank and Mabel Dodds, were relatives who opened their home to me. I could stay there overnight when I had play practice or other activities. Their house was an easy walk from school.

My best friend, Nina, and I spent hours together. We had many interests in common. Freda was another good friend. I did better in one-to-one friendships than in groups. Another good friend, Jane, came to our school as a senior, which is not an easy thing to do. We got along very well, and I've kept in touch with her. She married a classmate, Dick, so we stop in to see Dick and Jane when we visit Mercer.

In eighth grade there was an incident that puzzled me. Every year a boy and a girl were chosen by their classmates and teachers to receive the American Legion Award. Nina was selected, but the Legion refused to give the award to a Jehovah's Witness. Although having different religions was a handicap to a close friendship as we matured, we kept in touch. I'll always value our friendship, and think of her with great affection and gratitude.

Eventually I got used to my body during my teenage years, not that I liked it much. I had a bad case of acne, and my teeth were crooked, and there was no hope of having them straightened. But I usually had clothes that I liked, except the ugly tan stockings. I tried to get away with ankle socks, but my mother said my legs would be too cold. All through school the girls wore skirts or dresses, no pants. In the lower grades during the cold winter months we had to stuff our skirts into snow pants.

I was never a social success. I did go to school dances, but never dated anybody at school. I went to a youth fellowship at another church,

42

and did go out with a few of the guys from there. We often went to square dances. Sometimes I would go with a group of other 4-H members to big meetings at Penn State. I didn't realize that while girls were thinking about how cute a guy was, the guys were also thinking "cute," but mostly about sex. Fending off unwanted advances was part of the routine. I didn't know about homosexuality. But I dated one fellow who just didn't act like other boys. Even then, I got the idea that he liked the other fellow on double dates more than he liked the girls. Something just wasn't right. I had a number of early marriage proposals, and I always thought, "Huh? I'm certainly not interested in that."

World War II

The year that I was in sixth grade was when Japan bombed Pearl Harbor. Japan? We had always read nice little stories about beautiful Japan and their charming customs. But now they became the hated Japs or Nips, and the world changed completely. On the West Coast, Japanese-American citizens were taken from their homes and businesses and put in internment camps. A Sonoma friend was one of the internees when she was about four years old.

I think it's impossible now for younger people to realize that WWII affected every citizen of this country. A physically-fit male's only choice was which branch of the military, and often not even that choice. "Greetings" from the government were sent to 18-year-old boys, if they hadn't already enlisted when 17. The recruiting offices were flooded with volunteers, because support for the war was very nearly universal. In Art's high school graduation class there were two 4-F guys, and all the rest had already enlisted or been drafted. The only boys still in class, besides the 4-Fs and those not yet 18, were like Art, already in the service, and would leave immediately after graduation.

A younger person wouldn't know what "4-F" means. At a recruit's physical exam, if he could see, hear, and walk, he probably passed, but being 4-F meant he was deferred from service. Flat feet earned that designation. Other deferments were for age and for special family and/or job responsibilities. Ratings went from 1-A to 4-F.

I remember that every magazine ad had the men shown in uniform. Women, too, volunteered for service as WACS (Army) and WAVES (Navy). Women were also in the air service. They ferried planes between locations. Civilians, both men and women, were heavily involved in the war effort in every phase of life, from building ships to entertaining the troops. "Rosie-the-Riveters" became a war hero. Many women became expert welders.

The war effort affected every part of our lives. Many things were rationed: sugar, coffee, meat, cheese, butter, shoes, tires, and gasoline. I put my name on a waiting list for my first pair of nylons. There wasn't a cigarette shortage. Smoking was widespread and common. Cartons of cigarettes were also used for cash or barter, especially overseas.

We contributed scrap metal and even bacon grease, which was used in explosives. We bought war stamps every week. Enough stamps would grow into a war bond. There was a huge effort by movie stars and others to urge us to buy war bonds, which financed the war.

There weren't any new cars. Tanks were rolling off the Detroit assembly lines. Ships and planes were produced instead of any consumer goods. People from all over the country went to California for wartime jobs. Members of the armed services often passed through California on their way to overseas assignments. They liked what they saw on the west coast and many decided to settle there after the war. The population growth led to changes in California culture and politics, such as farmland becoming home sites and businesses, and a Republican state turning Democrat.

J. M. Flagg's 1917 poster, based on the original British Lord Kitchener poster of three years earlier, was used to recruit soldiers for both World War I and World War II. Flagg used a modified version of his own face for Uncle Sam, and veteran Walter Botts provided the pose.

During the war, our Current Events studies at school were largely about the conflicts in both Europe and Asia. Families displayed a blue star in their window to honor a family member in the service. Too often that blue star changed to gold as another life was lost. Our family was fortunate in not losing anybody, but we all knew of "gold star mothers" who had lost their dear children. Many soldiers passed through a local camp on their way to active duty. Later the camp was used for German war prisoners.

So at the same time I was going through my puzzling and worrisome teen years, the terrible war was causing untold suffering all over the world. We read of D-Day and the unbelievable slaughter on the Normandy beaches. The fierce battle of Midway was a turning point in the war in the Pacific. My 1944 scrapbook is a treasure of news stories from the year when the Axis was finally being defeated. But it was defeated with such a loss of life and treasure. A million British citizens were killed or injured in the conflict. Add to that the other Allies, the enemy combatants and civilians, and the Jewish people who were killed in Nazi death camps.

President Roosevelt died in April 1945, after serving only a few months of his fourth term. The surrender of Germany came less than a month later. Vice President Harry Truman was the new president. It's hard to believe that he hadn't been told about the Manhattan Project and the development of an atomic bomb. Now he was faced with the decision of whether or not to use the bomb.

An invasion of Japan was imminent. Truman consulted with military and government leaders and was told the prospects for invading Japan. House-to-house combat was likely with enormous loss of life on both sides. Thousands of lives had already been lost in the fierce battles for small Pacific islands, and what would an invasion of the homeland be like? However, debate still rages about the wisdom of dropping the bombs. Hiroshima was the first target on August 6, 1945. A second bomb was dropped on Nagasaki three days later, and six days after that Japan unconditionally surrendered.

I was fifteen then, and I remember the wild victory celebrations. I'm usually not with the mood of the crowd, and I wasn't then. I felt sorrowful about the terrible things that had happened as countries tried to kill each other. I felt more like crying than celebrating. I'll never know if other people also had the mixed emotions of glad and sad at the end of the war, or if it was just another example of teenage weirdness.

◀ ❙ ▶

PART TWO:

ARTHUR IRVING COOPS
AND
SHIRLEY SHANNON COOPS

ANOTHER FORK IN THE ROAD

The war was finally over. Women who had been working in defense factories, the Rosie-the-Riveters, went back home. G.I. Joes came home, too, and together they started to produce impressive numbers of babies. I was still in high school, but in 1948 I graduated as salutatorian in a class of about 50. I was a combination of competence and ineptness. Taking tests, writing papers, and even talking in public weren't problems. But I didn't feel comfortable in social settings. On the world scene, the United Nations established the country of Israel in the Middle East. In South Africa apartheid was begun. The stage was set for all kinds of mischief.

Westinghouse Electric, 1948

My parents said there was no way they could afford college, so I started business school in Sharon, Pennsylvania. I didn't like it, and about a month later I applied and was hired by Westinghouse Electric Corporation's Transformer Division, also in Sharon. This was a large company with 11,000 employees. It was a bustling place as they tried to catch up with post-war demand. This location had a doctor and nurse on duty every day. Other signs of a profitable company were a full-time photographer, a limousine with a chauffeur, a receptionist who looked as though she was out of Hollywood casting, and two real live telephone operators with velvety voices.

My job was a file clerk since I had no special training. But I liked delivering prints all over the office. After about a year I was asked if I wanted to learn to run a payroll machine and I did. But I wish I had tried for a different job, because I didn't like sitting at a machine all day and not seeing any other people than those right around me.

At least two memorable things happened in those years. I acquired

49

a little Chevy coupe and I started dating a new guy. We had so much fun with square dances, movies, trips to Cleveland to watch the Indians play baseball, his softball games, and a few TV parties. Television was new and not many people had sets. I thought those TV parties were boring.

One Sunday we drove to Niagara Falls, which was about five hours away. It was a very long day but lots of fun. He was a wonderful companion, but I was concerned about making a commitment to be a farmer's wife after hearing 20 years of my mother's complaining about it.

One day in 1951 a friend at work asked me if I wanted to meet a guy in her office. He had broken up with somebody and his co-workers decided to make a list of girls that he could check out. I thought, "Why

Art and Shirley Coops,
May 10, 1952

not?" I asked his name and she said Art Coops. I said, "That's a funny name." Arrangements were made for us to meet in the hallway at Westinghouse Electric. I don't think either of us was blown away, but maybe cautiously optimistic. He asked if he could take me home and I said okay. I was in a car pool and cancelled my ride home.

Engineers had been hired from all over the country, but still I was surprised when he said he was from California. He didn't have a relative east of the Sierra, but he thought the job would be a good chance to see the East as he went through the Westinghouse student course.

Taking me home was a challenge because of the long snowy hill on the way to my house. His car got stuck and he had to put on chains for only the second time in his life. I thought, "This is an even-tempered guy." We continued to see each other. I liked meeting his friends and seeing a different world than the one I knew. I liked it, and I liked him. Now I was in the awkward position of dating two guys. Sometimes at work I would go to the restroom and sit there and cry. It was hard to break up with my farmer, but I found out that my engineer was a farmer at heart but didn't try to make his living at it.

We were married about a year later in May 1952. We had a nice little ceremony in my church. My sister was my attendant. My father walked me down the aisle and my mother looked happy and proud. The reception was in the church basement. My friends and relatives came, and our friends from work. Art's folks couldn't manage the trip, but we would be seeing them in California. The wedding was on one of the rainiest evenings we ever had in Pennsylvania.

After the ceremony and reception we went back to my house and I got ready to leave on a three-week road trip to California. In those days a "going-away outfit" was part of the custom. It was even part of the newspaper write-up. I had a beautiful navy blue suit and a fancy hat and gloves. My sister thought it was hilarious when I was sitting there in the car all dressed up and trying to look dignified as our car died because the guys had messed with something in the engine. Why did I get dressed up and carefully straighten my stocking seams when we were just going to a motel in Ohio? Customs of the day make people do strange things.

Since I hadn't been west of Ohio I was so happy and excited to be taking a trip to California. It was a wonderful trip, even though there were no Interstates yet and most of the way we were on two-lane highways that went through many little towns. Traveling on Route 66 was a special treat. Not so much fun was one day when I was driving and was alarmed to see a car drifting into our lane and coming right at us and there was nowhere to go. I blew the horn and the driver woke up. We had to pull over for a while to calm down.

Something else that was scary was getting closer to Art's home town of Sonoma. Would they like me? Evidently they were willing to give me a chance. Art's lovely Aunt Dorothy and dignified Uncle Harry, along with Art's sweet and friendly sister, Betty, hosted a reception for us. It was a little confusing to have the relatives call Art "Irving." His father's name was Arthur so he had always been called by his second name. But at Berkeley in the Navy V-12 program, he found that everything had been set up for Arthur Coops and since he liked that just as well he didn't fight it.

The California visit was soon over. On the way home, just as on the way out, we stopped at many beautiful parks and scenic spots.

I found that Art was an enthusiastic tourist. He read all the his-

51

toric plaques and picked up the information that was offered. I wrote in my journal about the new experiences. I was slightly giddy with all the dramatic changes in my life. We got along fine spending 24 hours a day with each other, which perhaps is a test that not all couples could pass.

We arrived safely back in Sharon. As we came into the city I thought that the colors looked dull. But we were home and we had a little apartment on the other side of town. We happily went about settling in. I didn't have any role models for being a working wife. I made it more difficult than it needed to be. I tried to do things as they had been done at home. Perking coffee and getting a big breakfast and cooking and baking from scratch put a strain on getting to my job on time. Routines that worked on the farm weren't successful now. I had trouble fitting my two jobs together. But we were ready to start a family so I wasn't planning on working very long.

That fall I was 22 and eligible to vote in my first presidential election where I voted for Dwight D. Eisenhower, the five star general who commanded the invasion of Europe in WWII. Now the "police action" in Korea had been going on and people weren't happy about it.

I liked our little apartment and our life there, even though I didn't feel confident about how well I was succeeding with the cooking and laundry. One of Art's co-workers and his wife, Harry and Ethel Kaul, were good friends. They were westerners from Reno and perhaps that's why Art found them to be special friends. Ethel was a mentor to me. I was suddenly with mostly college-educated people, and sometimes I felt my lack. She was so helpful in guiding me through experiences that were new and challenging.

BUILDING AND FEATHERING A NEST IN THE 1950s

Ababy arrived before our first anniversary. However, it wasn't my baby. At age 45 my mother gave birth to a healthy red-haired baby boy that she named Michael. This was in March 1953. Before the baby came my father looked at the tiny clothes and just shook his head. My parents, friends, and family were all surprised. One acquaintance asked my mother why she always had my baby with her. My sister was a senior in high school. She enjoyed helping care for the baby. I remember watching him in our apartment.

Brother Michael
Shannon, two, 1955

My parents had been married for 24 years, and my mother was still living with her mother-in-law. To this day, my sister and I talk about what might have brought some peace to the family. That question will never be answered. Mother's mother-in-law, our dear Grandma Shannon, was 93 by now and in good health for that advanced age. She worried about who would take care of her. My father, an only child, took the responsibility seriously.

My sister,
Dorothy Shannon.
Mercer, PA
High School, 1953

I never had a mother-in-law since Art had lost his mother at an early age. I always had my own home. We had an apartment first and then built a house in 1954. Art chose a plan that he liked but I thought it was far too expensive. Mortgages scared me, and I thought, incorrectly, we could get a bigger house when we needed one. I got my way, but didn't know my husband well enough to recognize that, for him, when something is done, it's really done. Art agreed to a smaller house, and we took out an $11,500

53

Veterans Administration loan at 4½ %.

It was very exciting as the house took shape, and in about four months we moved in. Art had already started his garden on the property, which was several acres. Soon there was an orchard and then strawberry plants, raspberry bushes, and grape-vines. I was foolish to think that we would ever move and leave all that.

Melinda (1 month) & Shirley

In 1955, my sister drove to Arizona to marry her Air Force fiancee, Ray Walker. The following year our 3-year-old brother, Michael, became an uncle when Dewey Grier Walker was born. He was named af-ter his grandfathers, Dewey Walker and Grier Shannon.

Our hoped-for baby hadn't arrived, and I discovered I had a problem that required surgery. This was successful, and our first baby, Mary Melinda, was born in July 1956. I thought she was by far the cutest baby I'd ever seen, even though she didn't have much hair. I called her "little sweetie." My grandma, now failing, was happy to see the baby. Grandma died soon after, at age 97. Finally, my mother had her own home after 28 years of marriage.

Things were going nicely at home, but there was turmoil at the Westinghouse plant. The union called for a strike. Top management, although not all the department heads, took a belligerent attitude and started a "back to work" movement. They wanted to break the union. This opened wounds that never healed, and labor relations were poor from then on. The office workers weren't directly involved in the strike but were greatly affected by decisions made by top management as a result of the strike. The new policy proclaimed that not all transformers would be made in Sharon. Westinghouse would expand into other locations. This was the beginning of the end, not only for the highly successful Sharon transformer division, but for the corporation as a whole. But for now, jobs continued as they had been.

We hadn't visited California for six years, so in 1958 we took our two-year-old on a plane trip. Actually, it was my first plane trip, too. It was a prop plane so was quite a long noisy trip. We were all dressed up, as people did then for plane travel. Melinda wore her little white gloves most of the way.

Art's dad was very happy to see his granddaughter. His last six years had been eventful, too. Since he had lost the children's mother at a young age, and had been unmarried for nearly 25 years, we were pleased when he married a lovely widow, Esther Morris. He sold his bottled gas business and his Sonoma house, and bought a 47-acre prune/walnut ranch in Kenwood at the corner of Sonoma Highway and Greene St. Melinda was a good little tourist. We went to the Coast, visited San Francisco, toured Sonoma, and visited various relatives. Melinda immediately accepted Esther as another grandma.

Dad Coops and Esther-1956

The Kenwood House

We all enjoyed Dad Coops' and Esther's big house. I hadn't been impressed with the pictures Dad Coops had sent. The house looked so bare and rather foreboding. But Esther and her daughter-in-law had a way with plants and they had planted and nurtured beautiful landscaping. Now the house was lovely inside and out. The dining room was large and the walls were paneled with Australian eucalyptus. The entry hall was also paneled and had columns at the entries to the front parlor and also to the big living room.

The staircase was beautiful with a landing before it proceeded up more steps. There were four bedrooms plus a sun porch. Each bedroom had an individual sink behind an attractive narrow door. These sinks somewhat alleviated the problem of having only one full bath. The wrap-around front porch was an attraction. It could comfortably accommodate about thirty people. Off the kitchen there was a large back entry hall with a sink. A maid's room was also there, and a powder room. Steps led down to the large basement.

We saw Art's older sister, Betty Hammond, and son Bobby who lived in Richmond. Betty was a nice sister-in-law. She had suffered a tragic wartime marriage, but did get Bobby, a son she adored from the moment she saw him. Art's younger brother, Melvin, worked at the Lawrence Livermore Lab. His work was his life. He was in the Pacific for some of the experimental nuclear explosions.

Melinda (5) and Dinah (1 1/2), 1961

When Melinda was about three, another baby daughter, Dinah, arrived. I don't know why I expected her to look just like the first baby. But of course Dinah really was very cute with her own face and personality. Two small girls kept me busy. I tried nursery school for three-year-old Melinda, but she was very unhappy there. When she was four she was ready to go.

Art was a good daddy. He wasn't at all a domineering father, but not a push-over either. He often took the children out for walks or whatever else was going on out there. I have pictures of Melinda weeding the flowers when we got home from one of our trips.

Road trips were easier now with the new Interstate system. President Eisenhower believed that a better highway system was necessary for national defense. We watched the highway construction with great interest. We would go to watch new projects, especially something as spectacular as the Emlenton, Pennsylvania bridge on route 80. Cloverleaf intersections, overpasses and underpasses were amazing. We had never seen anything like it. We did have the Pennsylvania Turnpike, a forerunner of the new superhighways. The 1950s were blessed with prosperity and low inflation. There was an economic downturn in the late 50s, but Art's job didn't suffer.

◄◄ | ►►

A GROWING FAMILY IN A CHANGING WORLD, THE 1960s

The United States had come out of WWII as an undisputed world power. The Soviet Union flexed its own muscle all over the world and the Cold War was underway. Fidel Castro had taken over in Cuba. When the Soviets launched Sputnik, their achievement raised cries of alarm in this country. Now young, Catholic John F. Kennedy was the new president. He was elected in 1960 with a promise to "get the country moving again."

I wasn't aware that we weren't moving in the 1950s. I had a home with a husband and two beautiful little girls. We had a black and white television set, and we watched the popular shows of the day, including *I Love Lucy, Leave it to Beaver,* and *The Ed Sullivan Show.* We had TV dinners, Jello molds, Dr. Seuss, Dr. Spock, and American cars with fins. Most mothers stayed at home to raise their children themselves. A large percentage of people always went to church. All was right with the world.

But there were clouds on the horizon. Rosa Parks had decided there was no reason she should sit in the back of the bus. There was that pesky Castro and the matter of Sputnik. President Kennedy pointed out Viet Nam on a map. Communism was on the march there, too? The president directed an invasion in Cuba, but was defeated at the Bay of Pigs fiasco. He also had to cope with the missile crisis in Cuba, which led the Soviets and U.S. to the brink of war. Generally the people were inspired by the charismatic president and his glamorous wife, Jacqueline, and their two children, John-John and Caroline. When the president said we would put a man on the moon, the response was, "Let's get at it."

In our family's life in 1961, it was time to visit California again. Dad Coops and Esther were so hospitable. We didn't have time for all of our usual local touring because Dad Coops had made reservations at Yosemite. Art's sister, Betty, her new husband, Ed James, and our nephew, Bob, were able to come, too. Esther was a bit worried about riding to Yosemite with the four of us, but it was okay. At that time the rangers still pushed fire over the cliff, the famous fire-fall.

One night Dinah got stuck between her bed and the wall. She was not yet two and this was a lot of traveling.

We drove back to Kenwood, and soon it was time to go home. Dad Coops took us to the airport. He drove fast up and down the San Francisco hills, and the two little girls threw up their breakfasts, which included grape juice. This necessitated a change of clothes in the airport restroom. We flew to L.A. and visited the still new Disneyland. Flying on jet planes was new, too. Art was so calm about everything, which was very good because sometimes I felt nervous about everything. I don't think the girls suffered any permanent damage, even though one of the Disneyland rides was very scary for them.

In 1963 President Kennedy was assassinated. People remember where they were when that happened. I was painting a kitchen wall. My incredibly cute baby, six-month-old Alison, was in a little seat nearby. This was a pattern for the 1960s; personal happiness alongside the tumultuous events in the country and the world. Dr. Martin Luther King was leading a peaceful revolt against racial injustices. The Soviets had built the Berlin Wall, which divided that city. Lyndon Johnson, who had become president when Kennedy was killed, ordered an escalation of the war in Viet Nam. This led to huge anti-war demonstrations.

Alison, about 9 months, early 1964

One tragedy followed another. After the president's assassination, his brother, Robert, who was campaigning to be president, was murdered after a campaign appearance. Dr. King was shot and killed. The 1968 Democrat Convention in Chicago was a scene of riots and disruptions.

But in our comfy home we were doing peaceful things such as watching "Get Smart" and "Gilligan's Island" on TV. I was so busy with our three little girls that I hardly had time to keep up with the national news. It was a time of transition in many ways; fashions, makeup, dancing, and music of the day had all changed dramatically. There was a revolution

58

in birth control with the invention of the Pill. The Woodstock Music Festival in a muddy field in New York and the "Summer of Love" in San Francisco were beyond my understanding. The numerous children produced in the 1940s and 1950s, the Baby Boomers, were shaking things up.

Traditional events were happening, too. In 1965 we went to the World's Fair in New York City. I remember the IBM "People Wall" and exhibits by many other large American companies. People still bought mostly American cars, and

New York World's Fair
Art and Girls, 1965

the car companies had marvelous entries. Somehow we managed to ride the subway and make our way around New York with our three young children.

Danny Dec. 1966

Later that year, along with my mother and my twelve-year-old baby brother, Michael, we drove to Detroit to visit my Uncle Frank Weber and family. Aunt Vera was a good cook, and I very much enjoyed the meals there. Later I thought they were the best meals I was to have in quite a few months.

Morning sickness? Pregnant? I'm the woman who had trouble getting pregnant. Everybody, even our pastor, thought it was funny. I thought we already had our three and that was enough. But in 1966 we had four when Daniel arrived. It was very nice to have a boy, especially such a cheerful little fellow.

Each time we visited California we brought one more baby. Sometimes I wonder if they were all that pleased to hear that we were coming again. In years that we didn't go to California, we took trips to

59

other states. Eventually we hit all 48 contiguous states. We did much of this traveling in four-door sedans without air-conditioning. Art wanted to see the country and especially the National Parks. This was fine with me, but I'm not sure that the children were always happy with our vacation plans. However, they were wonderful little travelers.

The prosperous area around Sharon in western Pennsylvania was a good place to raise a family. Once Dinah said, "We have a nice little mall and a nice little dam with a lake." The schools did become crowded and Melinda sometimes had 40 children in her classes. In fourth grade she encountered a class and a teacher that weren't good for her. But she continued to do well. Dinah's artistic talent was evident at an early age. For second grade open house, Dinah's teacher had asked the children to make full-size paper cutouts of themselves to "sit" at their desks. Dinah's teacher said, "That really looks like her, doesn't it?"

There wasn't a kindergarten so I car-pooled with other mothers to take our children to classes for four-year-olds and then to private kindergarten. Alison always did extremely well with her schoolwork, and I probably took it too much for granted when she consistently had A's in almost everything.

Those were busy years. Besides school activities there were also programs for children at church. One friend and I were in car pools together for more than ten years. The Sixties had national upheavals but our lives were mostly routine. We celebrated birthdays and holidays, often with my parents, little brother Michael, and my sister and her family. I especially remember Christmas time when we always had freshly-cut Christmas trees that were invariably short fat ones that were more like big bushes.

It was the end of the Sixties and the beginning of teenagers.

A DIFFICULT DECADE, THE 1970s

Leisure suits and platform shoes didn't do much harm, but the Vietnam War was devastating. It seemed as though the whole country, family by family, was being torn apart. Sons and daughters turned against their parents. Older people thought that a "domino effect" was spreading Communism country by country, and the U.S. must take a stand in Vietnam. Younger people, especially in colleges and universities, were burning draft cards and holding numerous peace demonstrations and protests.

There were disagreements in our family, too. Melinda got contact lenses and the braces off her teeth and suddenly was beautiful. This opened up a new world for her. It was healthy growth, but it seemed to me that she became a different life form, and I was puzzled about how to handle it. She was still her kind helpful self, and completely trustworthy to watch the children and take care of little Danny. But she was also influenced by the "hippie culture," which had its own music, clothes, and mind set.

In 1972 Dad Coops' wife, Esther, died after 17 years of marriage. This was a great sadness for the whole family. That same year my own mother died unexpectedly from what was probably a cerebral hemorrhage. She was sick only a few days. She made an appointment with the doctor, but died during the night. She was 64, and the first of the eight Weber children to pass. Her childhood rheumatic fever may have damaged her heart. She had high blood pressure, not always well controlled, and she suffered the constant frustration of wanting her own home. We'll never know the exact cause of death. I was in shock for quite a while after she died.

Our family had another concern. At Danny's pre-kindergarten medical check-up, the doctor found a heart abnormality, a coarctation of the aorta, which would require corrective surgery when he was older. The year 1974 wasn't a good one. I had gradually taken on more responsibilities at church, and they were catching up with me. I was a Deacon, which meant I was to visit the sick and elderly. I had agreed to be a co-chairman of the Bazaar, a very large project that cleared over $10,000. There was my Sunday School class, too. I would have enjoyed each job, but not all at once. I was also called for jury duty that year.

Danny had regular check-ups at Children's Hospital in Pittsburgh. We found that they were doing the corrective surgery at younger ages. He was eight, and we should schedule his operation. He was so brave through it all. His surgery wasn't as early in the day as scheduled, because there was emergency surgery on a baby who needed the same open-heart operation. When his was finally over, we saw Danny in the I.C.U. with all the attached tubes. I asked how he liked getting to be the "Six Million Dollar Man," a popular TV series of the day. He said, "Not so great."

I was able to stay at the hospital all the time. The little heart patients did remarkably well, and they were able to eat full meals very soon. Many cases were complicated, such as the heart's connecting veins and arteries being reversed. It was a struggle for both the children and their parents. We were there for ten days, and Danny got stronger every day. It was remarkable surgery, and I remember the doctor's name, Dr. Sievers, from Texas. It's interesting that the whole thing cost only $4000, and Westinghouse paid for it.

I'll always wonder if the anti-nausea medicine I took during pregnancy caused the birth defect. There was some publicity concerning the drug's possible effects on the fetus, but nothing was ever proven. Fortunately I hadn't taken thalidomide. A friend had taken that drug during her pregnancy and her son was born with deformed hands.

Danny's surgery was in March, and we were able to go to church on Palm Sunday. I cried through most of the service. I was so relieved and thankful that the surgery was over and he was okay. The school supplied a tutor for a short time until Danny could go back to school. He recovered rapidly, and that summer we took a trip to South Carolina. Later in the year we went to Niagara Falls.

In the fall I had my regular doctor check-up. My blood pressure was up and my blood work showed irregularities. The doctor was puzzled and asked, "What have you been doing?" Stress was taking a toll on my body. The doctor prescribed medication and suggested that I slow down. It wasn't only our family that had been having difficult years. World events were challenging. OPEC proclaimed an oil embargo on the U.S., and long gas lines resulted. People could buy gas every other day, depending on whether their license number was an even or odd number.

Richard Nixon was re-elected president. His election had been pretty much assured, but it wasn't certain enough to satisfy him. Bit by bit information came out that there had been a burglary at the Democrat's Watergate office. The scandal following the cover-up dragged on for months, with Nixon's resignation as the result. Vice President Gerald Ford became president.

Things weren't going well in California either. Dad Coops had lost his wife, and now it appeared that he would lose his ranch. The prune/walnut orchard was old and not very productive. Expenses were overtaking income. Finally his banker said, "Don't you realize you're sitting on a gold mine in Kenwood?" So Dad Coops sold a few acres, and the buyer immediately resold it for twice the price, which made Dad Coops very angry. This opened his eyes to see that his situation wasn't hopeless.

Dad Coops now had enough money to take Farm Bureau's Farmer-to-Farmer tours. He took the film with pictures of his trips to be developed at a local drugstore, and struck up a friendship with an attractive lady who worked there. The lady, Cathryn Vallier, said she liked to travel and he said she should come along next time. She said she wasn't that kind of girl, so they got married. She was 66 and he was 77. Dad Coops continued to sell land during the 1970s. He and Cathryn were able to take a Carib-

Art & Cathryn Coops Dec. 1973

bean cruise, and trips to South America, Israel, and France. Dad Coops wanted to see the dock in France where he had done army duty in WWI.

The next time we visited California Cathryn was the lady of the house. She was our younger children's new grandma, but Melinda acted terrible. Cathryn thought she was a brat. Teenage brats aren't good, especially when they're in love and not happy about very much. It was years later that Melinda told me she missed Esther so much and was grieving for her. She saw Cathryn as an intruder

But it was mostly a good trip, the last one we would take with all four children. We drove across the country. We arrived in Kenwood in time to see the Fourth-of-July Pillow Fights. Visiting the Sonoma Coast is always a must and we spent a happy day there with our family— Dad Coops, Cathryn, and Art's brother, Melvin. Melvin usually came from his home in Livermore to Kenwood when we were there. Occasionally, he visited us in Pennsylvania.

San Francisco is an unfailingly fascinating city to visit, and this time was no exception. After leaving Kenwood we proceeded up the coast to Oregon where we visited Art's sister and her husband. On the way home we did the typical tourist stops including Mt. Rushmore. There we were astonished to run into our friends, the Amundsen family, from Pennsylvania.

One year Art had a business trip to San Francisco and I was able to go along. He and I had time to visit Dad Coops and Cathryn in Kenwood and also went to see a cousin in Santa Cruz. The trip was a nice change from routine family life.

When we got home Melinda prepared to go to college. Her high school graduation had been inauspicious, and at that time she said she'd had enough of school. She would get a job. But after a year of clerking, selling Avon products, and working at Burger Chef, she decided college might not be so bad. She was accepted at the Titusville, Pennsylvania branch campus of the University of Pittsburgh. Titusville was the site of the first oil well in the United States. The university buildings were fascinating. Many of them had belonged to oil millionaires. Even some of the old mansions were used. Melinda was more or less settled there for a couple of years and then was able to transfer to the main Pittsburgh campus.

My brother,
Michael Shannon

A pleasant short trip was to Pennsylvania State University to attend my brother's graduation in 1975. In 1976 we traveled with three children through the South and Southwest. We had a new Ford LTD, our first car with air-conditioning. We called it our "Bicentennial Car" because that was the same year our country celebrated its 200th birthday. This occasion was observed everywhere with parades and costumed pageants and

64

much flag waving.

By 1977, both Dinah and Alison were in high school. Their high school careers were easier on me than Melinda's had been. They weren't always happy with high school, but did enjoy parts of it. Alison continued her stellar scholastic accomplishments and also participated in music and sports programs, and enjoyed dancing lessons and recitals.

The winter of 1976-1977 was especially cold and snowy, which made it harder to get around. That was the winter that Dinah's choir group made hundreds of hoagie sandwiches that had to be delivered all over town. This project was to help fund the choir's trip to England. They did indeed get there for the year of the Queen's Silver Jubilee. They sang in their scheduled concerts and had time to go sightseeing. Dinah enjoyed seeing the Queen ride by in her coach. She thought Stonehenge was intriguing. A neighbor said she thought it was just a pile of stones. I thought it was interesting that Dinah had detected beauty and mystery there.

That summer we had our own Silver Jubilee when a friend hosted a 25th anniversary party for us. It was fun to have friends, family, and neighbors at the outdoor celebration. Our friends were superb hosts on

Shirley and Art Coops—25th Anniversary,
May 1977

that lovely summer day. Shortly after that we took a trip with only Alison and Danny. We saw the Air Force Academy's marvelous chapel. Another magnificent building was in Salt Lake City, the site of the Mormon Temple. The wonders of nature were all around us, too.

Our children's generation was growing up. In 1978 I hosted a bridal shower for my niece, Amy Walker. Many of my dear aunts were able to come. Meanwhile, Dinah was researching college and career possibilities. She liked art and she was interested in nursing and medicine, too. She heard about Medical Illustration, which would combine the two interests. Few schools offered this line of study, but the Rochester Institute of Technology in Rochester, New York, did. Dinah prepared her portfolio and sent in her application. Dinah always approached things with much emotion so when she was accepted we all knew she was happy.

In 1979 Melinda graduated from the University of Pittsburgh with a business degree. Melinda usually had more attention from men than she wanted, and certainly more than I wanted her to have. That year she

Back: Melinda, Dinah, Alison   **Front:** Art, Shirley and Dan
1979

asked us to come to her apartment to meet Michael Spring. He had been asking her out for some time, but she didn't want to go. One day he said she could at least have dinner with him because he had just received his doctorate, so she agreed. They began seeing each other regularly and now she wanted us to meet him. I thought it was probably just one more guy.

All the girls had enjoyed their dolls, and they fashioned ingenious little outfits for them. Boys are something else. Danny helped mow the lawn from the time he could barely reach the handle bar. He particularly liked digging and hoeing. From the time he was quite small he went down to the creek and constructed dams. He liked construction machinery toys and moved around a lot of dirt with them. One summer our neighborhood had a real construction project when a bridge was replaced. Danny spent much of the summer there. The workers even gave him his own hard hat. Our road was closed, and without any traffic it was a safe place for the children to learn to ride their bikes.

The children liked to grow pumpkins with Danny being the chief instigator. For several years we would have a dozen or more jack-o-lanterns lined up in front of the house. One year somebody came and smashed them all, which ended the multiple jack-o-lantern displays.

Dinah was able to take one more trip with us when we went to Florida, and then she was off to the Rochester Institute of Technology. The relatively new R.I.T. campus, about five hours away, was constructed of more bricks than I had ever seen in one place. We noticed that the Kodak Company was involved in many aspects of the school's operation.

A time or two, Dinah called and was in great distress. She said, "This is too hard. I can't do it." But she kept working and completed her freshman year. She found that Medical Illustration would require many years of training, almost as many as a doctor. Illustrations would be used for text books and instruction. Drawings had to be technically and artistically correct. Dinah changed to Graphic Arts. She didn't lose any credits because the first year was the same for either course.

For the summer of 1979 only 13-year-old Danny could go on vacation with us. Both Dinah and Alison had summer jobs. They missed the trip to Canada and new England. We went to Newport, Rhode Island, and toured several "cottages," the spectacular summer homes built by the very rich in the early part of the 20th century.

The last year of the decade was coming to a close. People weren't happy with President Jimmy Carter's time in office. Inflation and interest rates were very high. He did call attention to the need to conserve energy and was well known for turning down the heat in the White House and wearing a sweater. Unfortunately the progress that had been made in finding alternatives to hydrocarbons nearly stopped when oil again became reasonably priced.

Since my mother's death in the early 1970s, I had tried to provide a meal once a week or so for my father. In the late 1970s, my sister and her husband moved to his house so they could help him. My sister had always liked the farm and was happy to be there, although care-taking has its difficulties.

In the last month of the decade, we were in the usual Christmas whirl. Alison had many activities, including a dance recital and a party at our house for the cast of a school production. All the children were home for Christmas, and again we gathered around our Christmas "bush." A picture shows that it was one of our especially fat trees. We had a guest for Christmas dinner, Melinda's boyfriend, Michael Spring.

LIFE, DEATH, LOVE, MARRIAGE, IN 1980-1981

A rt and I both started to work at Westinghouse Electric Corporation in July 1948. I was at the Sharon, Pennsylvania, transformer division and Art was on the student course for eight months before accepting an offer to work at the Sharon plant. Transformer design was interesting and also was the most profitable Westinghouse division at the time.

We didn't meet each other until three years later. That wasn't surprising since there were 11,000 employees in the huge facility. It hummed night and day and cranked out thousands of transformers. There were customers world-wide. Profits were large enough to fund the new atomic division in Pittsburgh. It was believed that nuclear energy would provide so much cheap abundant power that electricity wouldn't even be metered.

The picture had changed completely by 1980. Bad management and bad timing combined to make the Sharon plant a shadow of its former self. Management had decided to greatly expand transformer production capability with new plants in Indiana, Georgia, Missouri, and Virginia. At the same time the post-war demand for transformers had been satisfied and orders fell dramatically. Art's job and salary continued but it was stressful to work in such an environment.

Our home life was good, unlike the turmoil going on at Westinghouse. Dinah was able to travel with us that summer. When we reached Washington we saw evidence of the eruption of Mt. St. Helens. On the road ahead of us volcanic ash swirled like a light snow-fall. We bought cherries, which the shopkeeper anxiously washed so they were ash-free. It was sad to see where Spirit Lake had been. The Toutle River was mud and destroyed trees.

We had an especially nice visit in Kenwood. Art's sister, Betty, was able to be there and we went to the County Fair in Santa Rosa and to San Francisco. We were surprised to agree that we had more fun at the Fair and its wonderful flower show than in the city.

Touring Gold Country was a special treat because Art's grandfather was born in that area during Gold Rush days. I was nervous on the narrow, dusty dirt roads. We tried to imagine life in those days when Art's grandfather, as a young boy, went across the mountain to get supplies. He had a donkey with storage bags over its back. He also carried a shotgun.

There was a small museum at a ranger station. Displays explained the environmental disaster that hydraulic mining had been. Water under great pressure washed away dirt so gold could be sifted out. The washed-away dirt went into the river, which then rose alarmingly. Finally the downstream farmers were able to get laws prohibiting this destruction.

Alison Coops–High school graduation, Hickory High School, Hermitage, PA   June, 1981

Home again, and Dinah drove back to the Rochester Institute of Technology in a little Pontiac Astre that we found for her. It was about that time that Danny became a more grown up "Dan." Melinda was working in Pittsburgh and she and Michael had decided to move in together. Alison had a busy junior year in high school. On the day of the SAT test, she had flu-like symptoms and didn't feel at all well. However, she scored high on the test and won a full tuition scholarship to Pennsylvania State University. She was chosen for a Westinghouse scholarship, too. When she came home from school one day I told her she had won. She sat down abruptly and said, "Oh, people will hate me!" Winning two scholarships was a joy and a burden.

The year 1980 was a mixture of successes and concerns. My father's diabetes was causing more trouble. Holidays that year were to be his last. In June 1981 Alison graduated from high school and was able to travel to California with us that summer. Dad Coops was bursting with pride about Alison's scholastic achievements.

Cathryn was a fun grandma. She agreed to play Scrabble with Alison and Dan. They expected an easy win but Cathryn beat them handily. She said she had cut her teeth on a deck of cards and she knew her games. She was quite an accomplished lady and at one time or another was Regent of the local DAR and president of the United Methodist Women.

The busy summer continued with a bridal shower for Melinda. I don't remember it but I have pictures. I do remember the August wedding. I wore the dress I had bought at Rosenburgs Department Store in Santa Rosa. My sister, Dorothy, said it was the nicest wedding she had ever attended. Dorothy's husband and children were there and, of course, all of our children. The wedding certainly was different. It was on the top floor of a Pittsburgh hotel. Michael was one of seven children, and his mother and his siblings and their children were all there. His father had died recently. It wasn't the Roman Catholic wedding that Michael would have preferred but he was happy.

Melinda's bridal picture (Mrs. Michael B. Spring) August 1981

Melinda, now age 25, was model-perfect in her wedding gown. We were happy that she was marrying a man well established in a career he enjoyed, which was being a college professor. He obviously adored Melinda. After the ceremony we gathered in a large dining room and waiters took our orders. The only clear picture I have in my mind of the reception is Melinda sitting on the floor and playing with a group of children. There was music. I lost track of popular music sometime in the 1950s and since then I don't know one decade's music from another's. However, if I hear 1940s and early 1950s music I still know many of the lyrics.

In September Dinah went back to R.I.T. and Alison started her Penn State career. She had wanted to be a teacher, but the education major had a poor reputation and she couldn't take the courses she wanted. She changed to finance.

As the girls settled into college, Dan into high school, and Melinda into married life, my father's health continued to deteriorate. His doctor thought an operation on his leg would improve circulation. It appeared that he was making a good recovery, but he took a turn for the worse and died in early October at age 78. I think he was the most honest person I ever knew. He treated everybody the same and wasn't intimidated by people in different social orders. Things are never the same after parents are gone. Sometimes parents are the only ones who care where you are and how you're doing. I'll admit that it felt strange to be the oldest generation now.

That same week the Pastor Emeritus, Dr. William Wishart, of our Presbyterian Church in Sharon also died. He had been our pastor for the first 17 of the 29 years we had attended that church. Many people said he was the wisest man they had ever known and I agreed. There were some wealthy and influential people in the church but he and his wife, Sarah, were always even-handed. Dr. Wishart's advice was practical as well as compassionate. The first time I saw him was when Art asked me to go to his church. Dr. Wishart preached about the years when Jesus taught and how he must have looked, the color of his eyes and hair, and what the land around him looked like. Jesus came to life and it touched me. It was the first time I had thought of Jesus in such a personal way. It was a religious experience that made me cry.

We started to hear about some unexplained deaths in the gay community. Whatever the disease was, it caused excruciating and certain death. Doctors and scientists were puzzled. It was the beginning of frantic study and research, which finally revealed that a virus, Human Immunodeficiency Virus, HIV, caused Acquired Immune Deficiency Syndrome, AIDS.

Between his sophomore and junior high school years Dan spent the summer with his first computer. Computers were soon to touch every aspect of our lives.

THE NEST IS ALMOST EMPTY, 1982-1983

The three girls were all within a five-hour drive. Melinda was living in Pittsburgh, Dinah at school in Rochester, New York, and Alison at Pennsylvania State University. In May 1982 we were proud parents as Dinah received her degree from the Rochester Institute of Technology. Since she didn't yet have a job offer she decided to check out the job scene in California. She stayed with Dad Coops and Cathryn for a month while she assessed opportunities. Her training in Graphic Arts in the east was a little different than that taught in California art schools, and employers were more receptive to California applicants.

Dinah's commencement Rochester Institute of Technology, May 22, 1982

We, with Dan, drove to Wisconsin where my brother lived, left our car there, and flew to Oakland. It was a delightful surprise when Dinah and Art's sister, Betty, met our flight. What fun to arrive for yet another sight-seeing/ visiting California vacation. Dinah flew back with us to Madison where we attended my brother's lovely little wedding when he married Marcia Solen.

Michael and Marcia Shannon
July 3, 1982

Home again, and we took Dinah to Rochester where she packed her car for a trip to New York City. She soon learned that a car wasn't needed there. It turned out to be eight-and-a-half years of valuable and sometimes exhausting work and social experiences. She said it wasn't easy to live in the city, but the time

73

spent there looked very good on her resume when she wanted to move.

We didn't know that we were about to move, too. Sharon's Westinghouse Transformer Division was very small now and we didn't know how we might be affected by the plant's slow but steady decline. One day I was at a luncheon at church and the church secretary found me and said she had a message from Art. He told her he had been transferred to Pittsburgh and we would have to move. There were gasps of surprise around the table as my friends heard the news at the same time.

We had lived in the same house for 29 years and hadn't planned on ever moving. Our little house had been crowded with four children but it was about right for us now. I couldn't believe we were leaving our house where we had raised the children, knew our neighbors, and entertained friends and family. But we had seen Westinghouse moving its transformer design and manufacturing to other locations so we knew we could be affected eventually.

Engineering and marketing departments were moving to offices on the west side of Pittsburgh not far from the Pittsburgh International Airport. Our house went on the market and we began a series of house-hunting trips to Pittsburgh. I came home from them with visions of metallic wallpaper, dark rooms, pink bathroom fixtures, and steps everywhere on the usually sloping lots.

We were resigned to paying more than we had planned until one day our agent said we could go along to an open house for realtors at a house just coming on the market. We walked in, and both Art and our realtor said they saw my face and knew that the search was over. The owners had redecorated most of the house and were still working on the lower level when they decided to move to Florida. I wouldn't have had the nerve to choose some of the wallpaper, but I saw it and liked it. The deal was closed almost immediately. Westinghouse handled the sale of our old house so we didn't need to worry about that. Moving allowances were generous. The moving van, some money for needs in a new house, and help with the 11% mortgage rate were all included.

It isn't necessary to go into the details of moving since most people are familiar with the experience of sorting and packing. Friends and neighbors had going-way parties for us and we left with sadness but also anticipation. I really liked our new house and the opportunity of living near a large city. Melinda and Michael had just bought an old

Victorian house on the east side of Pittsburgh and they were able to use furniture that we didn't need. Our new house was on the west side, which was convenient for Art's work.

The most difficult part of moving right then was that Dan was about to begin his senior year in high school and really didn't want to move. We managed to make arrangements with friends to let Dan live with them and finish school. They had to sign agreements to make it legal for him to stay. He stayed about three months with each of three families. It was a good experience in independence, because he had to take care of his own checkbook and appointments. It was somewhat like a first year of college. We provided a car for the necessary transportation.

Alison had a job that summer, but both she and Dan were able to go with us to New York City to see where Dinah was living and working. I liked the vibrant city activities with the endless possibilities for seeing things not available anywhere else. I remember we bought tickets at the World Trade Center to go to the Broadway show, "CATS." The subway, buses, and taxis made it easy to get around. Just walking was interesting, too.

Not so much fun was when we were at the top of the Empire State Building and I felt a sudden difference in the weight of my purse. I yelped when I saw a long-fingered hand in my purse and the hand was grasping my wallet. She (I think) let go of the wallet and melted into the crowd. I don't know what the person looked like. Dinah warned me to be more careful with my purse.

One day we took the cruise around Manhattan. When we got off the boat we saw women who were trying to pick up men. A scantily-clad young girl staggered out of a building. She was obviously under the influence of drugs. For Art these unfortunate parts of the city outweighed the advantages and he wasn't interested in going again.

We visited only once more. He preferred to send money for Dinah to come to Pittsburgh. She often did and sometimes brought friends. We made quite a few trips to the perfectly situated Frank Lloyd Wright creation, "Fallingwater," which he had designed for the Kaufman family. Dinah was fascinated with this masterpiece.

That same summer of 1983 before his senior year, Dan went to a class at Slippery Rock State College. He took himself there using his sparkly-new driver's license. Now all four children had their drivers'

Fallingwater

licenses and they were happy and we were happy that our drivers' education days were over. We got through it without mishaps.

Dan started his senior year with the Brown family. He called Dr. and Mrs. Brown mater and pater. We were so glad it worked out that he could finish high school with his friends.

PART THREE:

A GOOD MOVE AFTER ALL

A NEW AND EMPTY NEST, 1983-1986

In August 1983 the packers came and then the moving van. It felt strange to drive away from our home of many years while waving goodbye to our dear next door neighbors. That house was in western Pennsylvania and we drove 60 miles south to our new house near Pittsburgh. We stayed in a motel that night. For several months Art had been staying in the motel during the week so he could work in the new location and come home on weekends.

Now we had a home near his office. The moving van was able to park in the cul-de-sac overnight and was ready for the unloading in the morning. Melinda and Michael came and took some of our extra furniture for their new house. It didn't take long to put everything in place. It was only a week or so later when my brother, Michael, and wife, Marcia, came to visit. Marcia said she thought I would have everything put away and I did.

We had a nice visit, and could add some new activities for our company such as a river cruise around the three rivers; the Allegheny and Monongahela converge in Pittsburgh and form the Ohio River. Dinah came, too, and Dan was also with us. Everybody said they liked our house.

Occasionally I drove back to Sharon to visit with old friends there, and also to see my sister and family who lived on the old farm near Mercer. The barn burned down, which made me sad. So many memories were connected with it. It had sheltered our cows and horses and other animals. My father did the milking there. I remember that sometimes he would squirt the warm milk directly into the cat's mouth. We had "barn cats." They weren't anything like today's pampered pets. Our cats were workers that kept the barn rodent-free. We delighted in the adorable little kittens that arrived with closed eyes but soon were wide awake and ready for barn adventures.

Steps led to the barn's upper level. Outside entry was gained by going up the barn bridge, a wide graded approach to the barn floor. One side of the barn floor had graneries for oats and wheat. Haywagons were pulled inside so the hay could be stored in the haylofts that were on both sides. A track ran across the roof of the barn. There was an intricate arrangement of ropes and pulleys connected to a large pincher-type hay fork that grasped the hay, one bite at a time, lifted it off the wagon, raised it towards the roof, ran along the track and finally dropped it into the loft. Horsepower started this process by pulling the rope that lifted the hay fork. Sometimes I led the horse down the barn bridge. Some years later my sister used the tractor.

After hay balers came into common use that was the end of the cushy hay lofts. The hay lofts had been fun. We climbed up the built-in ladder, out onto the beam, and jumped into the hay. Once I fell backwards off the ladder and it knocked the wind out of me. The barn was a big part of farm life. I remember one July 4th the annual Ligo reunion was held in our barn. The barn floor was swept clean, tables were put in place, and dinner was served. The loss of the barn was the end of an era.

The fall of 1983 arrived and Dan settled into his home away from home with his friend and family for his senior year in high school. Alison moved into a new apartment at Penn State with a roommate that became a long-time friend. Dinah continued her New York City design career as she worked for several businesses. She endured teasing about her small-town look and mannerisms, but gradually acquired some big-city sophistication.

The holidays in our new house were fun. I decorated everything. We did quite a bit of traveling between our old location and our new. We attended Dan's school activities such as playhouse productions and cross country meets. The cross country friends were good guys, which was reassuring to us. He started to talk about going to Northwestern University. We said it was too expensive. When he visited the school in January we thought being in Chicago in the winter would change his mind but it didn't. He said he would join NROTC and that's what he did.

We were meeting new friends and neighbors. I also spent time with a cousin, Perle (Petty) Tallo Bliley, who lived in Pittsburgh. She and I went shopping and we celebrated our birthdays. We were just getting reacquainted when her husband was transferred. She liked to visit in person but wasn't a correspondent. She never answered my letters.

It was soon time for Dan's graduation, and we attended the outdoor ceremony. Rain threatened, but all of a sudden I had the feeling, "This is going to be fine" and it was. The senior year was successfully completed. We were ready to go on another California vacation.

We had always been able to use Dad Coops and Cathryn's car, but this time Cathryn said we couldn't because she did the driving now and didn't like to drive the pickup. Art's brother, Melvin, who lived alone in Livermore, offered to meet us at the airport and let us use his second car. We were at his house before driving to Kenwood. Alison and Dinah were able to come along and I enjoyed that. We saw Art's aunt and uncle and a couple of his cousins. Visiting San Francisco was a must, and along the way we stopped at the Marin Civic Center and Sausalito. Dinah left to go back to her work in New York but we stayed a while longer in the lovely Kenwood house before going back to Livermore.

Daniel Coops
Hickory H.S. Graduation 1984

After we got home, my brother Michael and wife, Marcia, came to see us, and to show us our new baby niece, Meghan. Now my baby brother had a baby daughter whose facial features were much like his.

In the next few years we visited towns that we wouldn't have except for our children's interests. Alison interned for IBM in Oswego, New York, and we also became acquainted with Evanston, Illinois, the home of Northwestern University. Dan packed in preparation for his first year there. He settled in his dorm and in the Navy, and was able to come home for Christmas, as were all the children. Melinda arrived alone and had been crying. As often happens with children I thought, "What now?" I was concerned, but she had never said much when anything was wrong and didn't that time either. She cheered up after being with her siblings for a while. It was a cold but sunny winter day and all six of us went for a walk at a nearby nature preserve. It was perhaps the last time that our nuclear family went anywhere alone together.

Melinda later said that Michael had ordered her to go get him some cigarettes. Michael was from a military family and giving and obey-

81

ing orders was the way his family lived. However, Melinda had received few orders in her life and the ones she did get she was more than likely to ignore. She was receptive to requests but not to orders.

Art's brother, Melvin, arrived for a visit in early 1986. He seemed to indicate that he would help pay for Dan's college, but it sounded as though it was conditional on Dan's taking the courses of which Melvin approved. Art abruptly left the room because he was afraid of what he might say or do. For now there weren't any serious points of dissension, but this was to change.

SETTLING INTO A NEW LOCATION

We had been disappointed about having to move but we soon found that we liked our new home in Moon Township. It was near the Pittsburgh International Airport, was convenient to stores and services, and had nice neighborhoods. At that time, the local government provided a "dump" where we could dispose of miscellaneous unwanted accumulations. After we had settled in we found that we already had such a collection so I took a load to the "dump."

A woman was there who was also unloading her car. She kept looking at me and finally said, "Are you a University Woman?" I had to answer no. I think she knew practically everybody in the area and was trying to make me fit. She asked, "Do you play tennis?" No, I still didn't fit into the groups where she might have seen me. Finally she asked, "Are you a Presbyterian?" I did answer that affirmatively and said we were new in the community. She invited me to church. She was wearing a shirt with a "Rochester" logo so I said that our daughter had just graduated from the Rochester Institute of Technology. She said her son was at the University of Rochester.

It was a happy coincidence that we were both cleaning out our cars at the same time. Lannie and Rod Gartner became good friends. They were both active in political and community affairs and told us about local opportunities. One was the Robin Hill Center, a refurbished mansion, that had become a gathering place for various activities. Lannie and I went to a Great Books discussion group every week. The extensive grounds had room for an herb garden, a small amphitheater, a cozy old log cabin where we occasionally had meetings and picnics, and a nature trail that was quiet and seemed far from human activity. Every year a festival was held in the mansion and on the surrounding grounds. Crafts, art, and food were abundant.

I met other women through the DAR, Daughters of the American Revolution. I had been wanting to pursue a membership and this was a good chance. They guided me through the documentation that I needed.

Mine was relatively easy because I could use my great aunt's DAR number and only needed the relevant birth, marriage, and death certificates for me and my parents and grandparents.

Another goal was to finish a quilt. I had always been fascinated with quilts. When I was about 12 I saw a newspaper ad that said I could send for a pattern with instructions for making a "Double Wedding Ring" quilt. I painstakingly cut out the many little pieces from my 4-H projects scraps and my mother's fabric collection. The

Shirley's first quilt

pieces rested in a shoe box for approximately 46 years. I decided to take quilting lessons and join a quilt club. Besides meeting many new friends, I finally finished that quilt and am still enjoying it. I went on to make quilts for the children and grandchildren. Wall hangings were smaller projects that I especially enjoyed. Occasionally our club raffled off a quilt for charity. One year we had just finished a quilt and sold raffle tickets. I got to pick a name out of the basket. I gasped when I looked at the name and read "Alison Coops." Alison was lucky as well as smart.

Alison graduated from Pennsylvania State University in May 1985. We went to a special "Scholars' Ceremony" as well as the impressive graduation for everybody. Afterwards she posed with the Nittany Lion sculpture and officially ended her studies at the school. She had been interning during the interview sea-

Alison Coops - Pennsylvania State University graduate, 1985

son, but did find a job about a month after graduating. She was hired by Ross Perot's company, Electronic Data Systems.

84

Dan was free that summer so with him doing much of the driving we headed for Arizona and California. Our niece, Cindy James, was getting married to Wayne Mundt in Bullhead City, Arizona, and we went to the wedding. It was a delight to have Art's cousin and his wife, Harry and Marguerite Van Coops, from Lompoc, California, there, too. They went with us from air-conditioned car to air-conditioned church to air-conditioned motel. The temperature in the sun was about 120 degrees. We were able to spend time with Art's sister, Betty, and her husband, Ed James, and also Cindy's brother, Bob Hammond, wife Karen, and their son, Bryan.

Catherine (Caddie) and John Melendy 1986

Harry and Marguerite Van Coops invited us to come to their home in Lompoc, and we had a good visit there. Then on to Soquel, California, to visit with Art's cousin Catherine Melendy and husband John. Several hours to the north was Kenwood and we spent the usual happy time there. Dan had enjoyed the visiting and had been very patient but he was ready to go home. We crossed many states quickly and soon were in Wisconsin, where we visited my brother and family. In practically no time at all we were back in Pennsylvania.

While we'd been gone Alison had packed her car and a U-Haul and gone to Plano, Texas, near Dallas, to begin training for her job. She thought Perot was a good boss and he encouraged and helped his employees to further their education. She was in Plano for five months, then to Bethesda, Maryland for four months, then to Michigan, back to Plano and finally to Rockville, Maryland. She decided after a couple of moves that she really didn't need a trailer full of stuff and made do with a roof-carrier.

Dan was quite dashing in his Navy uniform and was ready to begin his second year at Northwestern University. He had survived boot camp and was able to go on a nuclear submarine cruise. But this didn't solidify his decision to become a seaman. He talked to his commanding officer and they agreed that the Navy wasn't the right career for him. This presented a dilemma because of the high cost of the school, and we investigated other possibilities, none of which were satisfactory. Dan said he could get a job at school and he could also intern during the summers. He started his second year at Northwestern.

We spent Thanksgiving with my sister and her expanding family. She had several grandchildren now. All our children including Melinda and her husband, Michael, came home for Christmas. Toward the end of the Christmas break several of Dan's high school friends came and he went back with them to visit our old home area.

Winter was fading and spring unfolding. Good news of the season was when Melinda told us that she and Michael were expecting a baby in late September. Our first grandchild! That was exciting.

That same spring we visited Alison, who was living in a condo in Bethesda, Maryland. Dan went with us during his spring break. We enjoyed again seeing some of the famous Washington, D.C. sights. Dinah's college and New York friend, Grant Rector, came along when she visited us at Easter. Dinah had red hair! Not much surprised me now. It also wasn't surprising that they wanted to go to Fallingwater. It is a lovely place and I was always happy to go again.

Alison stopped by on her way from Bethesda to Detroit where she would have the next phase of her training. Melvin also visited when he came east on one of his business trips. Melinda invited us to their house for dinner. By now Melinda was wearing maternity clothes.

For the first time in many years we traveled to California without any children. Besides our usual family visits we also went to Mendocino County. Art's cousin, Will Coops, had done some family research and was able to locate an old cemetery called Cuffey's Cove Cemetery near Elk. He made a map for us to follow. Great Uncle August Volquardsen and two of his shipmates are buried there.

Back in 1897 the three of them were in a rowboat to take care of a problem with the ship. Due to a bad storm and the captain's poor judgment, they drowned. All three men's names are on one gravestone. Three cemeteries are in a row along this scenic spot on the Pacific Coast. The

Catholic Cemetery is the largest. The next is called the Druid Cemetery, and the third the Wayfarers' Cemetery where the seamen are buried. It didn't appear to be well maintained. We were fascinated by the spot and in a few years went back to see it again. The gravestone says August Volgerson, but it should be Volquardsen (b. 23 April 1865, d. 3 May 1897).

After more visiting and sight-seeing, we drove back to Melvin's home in Livermore. He was generous in allowing us to use his car and stay at his house when we needed to. He also provided transportation to and from the airport. There were occasional disagreements between the brothers, but the relationship was generally amicable.

THE CITY OF CHAMPIONS
GAINS ONE MORE

Pittsburgh's Golden Triangle is where the Monongahela and Allegheny Rivers come together to form the Ohio. It's called golden because of the vast amounts of money that were made in the steel industry. Pennsylvania steel mills supplied the steel for grand projects such as the Golden Gate Bridge and for basic products like cars and refrigerators. During WWII steel production was devoted to companies making planes, ships, tanks, and other war materiel. Many corporations were headquartered in Pittsburgh:

Shirley, Pittsburgh, 1987

U.S. Steel, Pittsburgh Plate Glass, Gulf Oil, Westinghouse Electric, Mellon Bank, and half a dozen other companies.

By the time we moved to Pittsburgh the air was clean because much effort had been put into creating a "Renaissance" of the city. Steel manufacturing is very dirty and it was said that sometimes streetlights had come on at noon because of the heavy smoke. Pollution controls, along with less steel making, made a welcome change.

It was hard and dirty work in the mills and in the early days there had been some bloody strikes as workers tried to organize. Eventually the United Steelworkers union became powerful, and the steelworkers earned very good money. Poor families, many of them European immigrants, became middle class. The city grew larger with towering buildings downtown. Many neighborhoods were built among the surrounding hills and valleys. The city was unusual in that neighborhoods were isolated from

88

one another. It was difficult to get around because there was always a river or a mountain in the way. Crime was low in these compact ethnic neighborhoods.

We enjoyed the benefits of money that had been spent in the past by generous steel barons and by the general prosperity of the area. The ornate railroad station had been converted to an elegant restaurant and a row of shops called Station Square. Andrew Carnegie's library and museum were points of interest. We visited Henry Clay Frick's mansion with its massive pipe organ. Phipps Conservatory's botanical collections were outstanding. There was a zoo and a planetarium. Many colleges and universities were in and around the city. The University of Pittsburgh and Carnegie Mellon were established early in the city's history.

A special treat was a ride on one of the inclines that ascended the cliff up to Mt. Washington. From there one could see both the rivers and the city. Once we had dinner at a restaurant that had windows along one side. As we ate it got dark and we could see the panorama of thousands of lights being turned on.

Every year there was an event called the Three Rivers Regatta. Two features that I remember were the "Anything That Floats Race" and the speedboat competition. Alison, with her ever-present car roof carrier, was in Pittsburgh for a visit as she moved between training sites. Some guy that she'd met came to Pittsburgh to see her. Back in the 1950s and 1960s when we produced three girls somebody said, "Never mind, the boys will come." Indeed they did.

We saw Melinda and Michael often. They converted the first floor of their old Victorian house for an apartment where Michael's mother could live. They lived on the second floor and were finishing the third floor for the baby. We also often went back to my hometown of Mercer and our old farm where my sister and her husband lived. I was still a member of my "Non-sewing Sewing Club." It had started with good intentions but had gradually lost that original purpose and was devoted to eating and chatting. I liked seeing the women that I had known for so many years while we were raising our children together.

Our new friends were nice, too. We met many folks at church and there was always plenty to do there. Art was an Elder and was involved in many aspects of church management. The worship services and music were important to us. I went to Women's Circle meetings and Art and I both went to couples' activities. I remember the progressive dinners when we went to different homes for each course. Sharing food for almost any reason is a feature of most churches. There was food for the soul, too,

with good Adult Education classes with interesting leaders. After a while we became aware of tension between different factions whose opinions of the pastor didn't agree. This wasn't good and resulted in the loss of some members.

On October 2, 1986, I received a call that Melinda had delivered a 9 lb. 9 oz. baby boy whom they named Jonathan Michael. I called Art at work and he went to the hospital and got to see the baby before I did.

Grandma Shirley & Jonathan, 1986

Melinda thought she was all ready for the baby's arrival, but found she wasn't ready for the emotional wallop that hit her. She was immediately enthralled with the adorable baby.

A new little champ had arrived in the City of Champions. The Steelers and Pirates had been making history, but for me Jonathan took precedence.

SHRINKAGE AND GROWTH IN PITTSBURGH

Pittsburgh was de-industrializing by the time Art was transferred there in 1983. The roaring blast furnaces were cold now and the numerous rolling mills were gone. Art worked for Westinghouse Electric Corporation, which had been founded in Pittsburgh but now it, too, was getting smaller as it sold off parts. Good paying jobs went with these industry cutbacks and the area lost population. Our children, along with many others, looked for careers in other areas.

The city was getting smaller but our family was still growing. Two high chairs were needed when we entertained 19 family members for Thanksgiving dinner in 1987. We had one-year-old Jonathan and my sister's newest grandchild, Jessica Burk. My brother and family couldn't come, but there was a new member in that family, too. We were surprised when they named their baby Zerlinna Shannon after our grandmother. There was a new Linna Shannon now. Melinda and Michael were expecting another baby. Holidays were special with the new little folks. It was so nice to enjoy them but not have to keep them.

Maybe it's time to confess how much I disliked all the paying jobs I ever had. From cleaning eggs when I was twelve to my years at Westinghouse Electric, I always thought I would rather be somewhere else. I found that "somewhere else" was getting married and having a family. Working mothers weren't the norm and my friends didn't have second jobs. The customs of the time often dictate behavior, and the economy was geared to one-income families. Some women would likely have been happier with jobs, and I think that some women now would be happier if they could stay at home with their children.

But then, with all our children out of the house I decided to try again, and I went to work at an office supply store on a three-week trial basis. I didn't like anything about it. Standing on my feet all day and receiving a pittance in pay wasn't meeting any needs at all. At the end of the three weeks I felt joyously free. I was almost skipping as I went shopping, got my hair cut, and felt like myself again. We had a new car, not that my job had anything to do with that.

I liked being at home because there was always something interesting to do. Even when I had the children's needs to meet I was still able to make my own schedule. If it had been necessary to have a paying job I'm not sure what would have been a good fit. I always enjoyed writing, even if it was just the minutes from a meeting. Once the associate pastor said that I didn't have to write a long flowery essay. Just the items for information and the items for action were required. Sometimes I wrote something special such as the guidebook for a house tour. I visited the homes, and the owners described what they planned to do for Christmas decorations. I enjoyed writing and assembling the booklet.

Besides the worship and music at church there were other activities such as sorting clothes for the needy and attending to the Food Pantry, which was held in the "Little White Church," the original church beside the big new one.

I was Conservation Chairman for our DAR chapter. Each year we selected a person for special recognition. I interviewed the candidates and, using a tape recorder, I wrote articles that were published in the local paper. One of the selected ladies told me that her friends said, "Oh, I didn't know you did all that!" I liked the patriotism and history connected with the DAR.

Another enjoyable activity was quilting, and my quilt club. I went every week. We had classes on developing further skills and I always learned something. We often went to quilt shows, and the skills exhibited there were impressive.

We looked forward to our children's visits. When Dinah came from NYC, sometimes with a friend, that usually meant another trip to Fallingwater. My brother and family stopped by as they made the move from Wisconsin to central Pennsylvania. He had been transferred to Amish Country, an interesting place to visit.

Pittsburgh always had something going on. Once a Mississippi river boat with all its old fashioned grandeur visited our rivers. We watched the supersonic French plane, the Concorde, arrive at the Pittsburgh airport for its first and only trip there.

Art and I took a walk almost every day. Any direction was nice.

We got extra exercise with our walking because it always involved hills. One walk was to an airport overlook. Pittsburgh was a US Air hub and planes came and went constantly. Neighborhoods were neat and tidy, and shopping was convenient. Art's gardening didn't work well on our city lot. When he did manage to grow something the chipmunks ate his strawberries and the rabbits ate anything green that came up. Art planted a couple of trees that did well, and the flowers were lush and pretty.

We liked traveling 60 miles north to our old home territory. We visited my sister and family, and also many of our old neighbors and co-workers. I sometimes went to see my friends at the non-sewing Sewing Club. We also traveled south to see Alison in Maryland where she was working for EDS. She introduced us to a man that she had met, Chuck Ludwig.

Dan brought a girlfriend to visit us in Pittsburgh, and even her parents came for lunch. This looked serious but it wasn't. I remember we took yet another trip to Fallingwater.

We went to California nearly every year. Sometimes Dinah or Alison could join us for part of the time. Art's brother, Melvin, greatly admired Alison and her talents, and we were troubled by what seemed to be improper attention to her. He acted like her boyfriend, not her uncle. He and Art had a not very friendly discussion about it. But mostly things were all right and we still used Melvin's Livermore house and his car. We tried to return his kindness with gifts and with hospitality when he visited us.

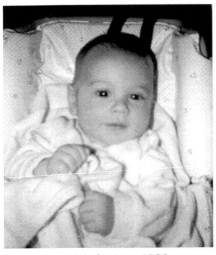

Patrick Spring, 1988

We were looking forward to the birth of a second grandchild. Besides taking care of their first baby, Jonathan, Melinda was looking after Michael's mother, who lived on the first floor of their old Victorian house. Mrs. Spring was in failing health and she died before Patrick Arthur Spring arrived on February 4, 1988. He was another big boy at 9 lbs., 2oz.

There were many trips back and forth across the city as we visited

93

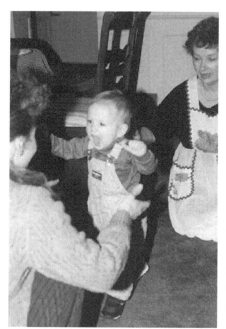
Melinda and Patrick Spring
with Grandma Shirley
January, 1989

the babies, and Melinda and Michael brought them to our house. We have pages of pictures of the very busy little boys and their very busy parents. Melinda and Michael took the boys to see their great-grandpa in California. I heard that the trip wasn't easy, but had its good moments.

Melinda invited us for Thanksgiving in 1988. Alison and Chuck were there, too. He also came with Alison for Christmas at our house. We were seeing this young man quite often. Dan was able to come, and also Melinda and Michael and their two little guys were there for Christmas dinner.

Melinda's family came for a big dinner at our house on New Year's Day, 1989. My brother and his family and my sister and her husband were also able to be there. A couple of weeks after that we watched Patrick take his first steps, such a fun milestone. Already the two little boys seemed to be surrounded by fleets of toy cars and trucks. They were ready to roll.

HIGHS AND LOWS OF 1989-1990

Alison met Chuck Ludwig at church. In a few months they were engaged and planning to be married in that particular Presbyterian Church in Germantown, Maryland. There was much planning to be done for the August 1989 wedding and reception. The clothes, the invitations, the food and music, and all the detailed preparations for a traditional church wedding. Alison and Chuck did most of the planning themselves so being mother-of-the-bride was easy for me.

Melinda and Dinah would be attendants for their sister, along with two of Alison's college friends. Dresses of deep turquoise were selected and the alterations made. Alison found a wedding gown to her liking. I chose a dress that was one of the prettiest I ever had. It was light pink with a fancy belt, and with the matching shoes and purse and sparkly earrings, I felt ready to do my part.

First was the rehearsal dinner, and we met Chuck's family for the first time; his parents, brother and two sisters and their families. Melinda and Michael had their two little boys who were only 1 ½ and not quite 3, adorable and a lot of work.

The day of the wedding, our lunch was at Chuckie Cheese and that was such a busy time that I had to hurry to get dressed for the wedding. The only thing I had to do at the ceremony was light our family candle. Mrs. Ludwig lit the one for

Alison and Chuck Ludwig,
August 26, 1989

their family. After lighting mine I turned to go back to my seat when I noticed people gesturing and pointing. My candle had gone out. I got to do my part twice. Everything else appeared to go just fine. After the

95

ceremony we shook many hands, smiled a lot, got our pictures taken, and proceeded to the reception hall where there was food and dancing. Then back to the hotel for some sleep until the next morning when we hosted a family breakfast. We had a couple of exciting days, but I breathed a sigh of relief when it was all over.

Dinah, Dan, and his girlfriend, Amy Ruhl, had driven to the wedding from New York. We hadn't met Amy before, and she told us later that she was glad she could meet us under those circumstances. Alison was the center of attention so Amy could stay well in the background.

The following month we flew to New York City to visit Dinah. She lived on the 15th floor of the building and the views were awe-inspiring. I enjoyed a few days of hustle and bustle, but a big city definitely wasn't Art's favorite place to be even though the sights and action were unique there. Dinah was gaining invaluable experience in her chosen field of graphic arts. I feel bad now when I look at the pictures of the World Trade Center towers and the page of pictures that we took from its height.

World Trade Center
Art and Dinah, 1989

The next month when we were watching the World Series being broadcast from San Francisco the screen suddenly went blank. We soon learned there had been an earthquake that caused considerable damage. Just a couple of weeks later Art had a business trip to the area and I went along. We saw evidence of the shaking from what they called the Loma Prieta quake. When we visited Art's cousin in Santa Cruz she showed us her collapsed chimney. We went downtown and saw the massive damage there. She said San Francisco got the publicity but Santa Cruz suffered, too. In the city we also had time to ride the cable car and see Chinatown, so there were bonuses to the business trip. We also saw Art's folks in Kenwood.

The busy year continued with Thanksgiving at our house. Newlyweds Alison and Chuck came, and also my sister and her husband,

96

and my brother and family. During these months I also had my quilting meetings, classes, and excursions, and various church activities. Once our women's group went on a luncheon cruise on one of the Pittsburgh rivers. Art and I often had visits with Melinda and Michael and their two always very active little boys.

Art was treated to a Westinghouse retirement lunch in December. However, that didn't mean he didn't go to work anymore, because he was then an independent contractor with Asea Brown Boveri, the Swiss-Swedish corporation that had bought the Westinghouse transformer division. He continued to do his same job as a design engineer.

Dinah and Dan came to spend some time with us at Christmas. We went downtown to see the Nutcracker, which was very nice, except I started to feel sick. Melinda and Michael came for dinner the next day but I didn't feel well enough to do much. The kids took care of dinner. I started to feel better but then got a back spasm that caused pain for a week.

Now it was the beginning of 1990. I thought I was fine, but one morning I looked in the mirror and the left side of my face was sagging. Stroke? The doctor said, "No, it's Bell's Palsy." What? I'd heard of it but didn't know what it was. Somehow the nerve to my eye and mouth had been damaged and the cause was unknown. I had to bandage my eye shut at night so it would stay closed. I couldn't say P or F, and couldn't sip from a cup so had to use a straw. It was very strange and scary. For several weeks I didn't want to go anywhere. As time went by it gradually improved. I've had two operations on my left eye to try to make it normal, but nearly twenty years later a new eye doctor was to take one look at me and say, "Did you have a stroke or Bell's Palsy?" Obviously the damage was permanent.

It wasn't a good winter or spring but I was healthy the rest of the year. Germantown, Maryland, where Alison and Chuck lived, and Lititz, Pennsylvania, my brother and family's home, were a convenient distance apart via the scenic Pennsylvania Turnpike. Lititz is in Pennsylvania Dutch country in the central part of the state where tourists come to observe the different style of life that's lived there.

There's also an Amish community in New Wilmington near my hometown of Mercer. Anytime we visited the old family cemetery we saw horses and buggies clip-clopping by. We liked being in the area and often shared good times with my sister and her husband who lived on the old homestead.

The rural part of the state is lovely but I preferred living near Pittsburgh for its conveniences and city activities. Highways were being built nearby to service the new Pittsburgh International Airport terminal. It was a principal US Airways hub then.

IBM had paid for Dan to get his master's degree at Cornell University in Ithaca, New York, and he graduated in May 1990. He had  studied Materials Science and Engineering Physics. We didn't know Cornell had such a beautiful campus and we enjoyed touring it. There was one area that had rock formations, a stream, and a picturesque bridge. The buildings were a combination of modern and traditional. One looked a little like a castle. The graduation ceremony was on a sunny afternoon and we were proud to see Dan in his cap and gown. He and Amy were a couple now and we sat with her.

Daniel Coops 1989
Northwestern Univ. Graduate

When we flew to California in June we didn't get to stay at the Kenwood house. Cathryn said it was too much for her to take care of and too far to drive to Sonoma for doctors, shopping, and church. At age 94 Dad Coops' sight and hearing were failing badly and there were some signs of dementia. They were living in a rented condo, a very pretty place. Dad Coops would have preferred staying in Kenwood but wanted to please Cathryn. She was 84 now and not sure she was up to another caretaking job. She had already taken care of her father-in-law and her first husband. But for the moment things were going all right.

◄◄ | ►►

PART FOUR:
STORMS AND CLEARING

THE GATHERING STORM

The time is coming when I'll need to recount the circumstances leading to our move to California. I've been puzzling about how to talk about our estrangement from Art's brother, Melvin. Art and his sister seldom thought about him after things were settled, so why I still hold this smoldering resentment is a troubling question.

My collection of devotional material has been sitting undisturbed and this is a good time to refresh my faith. Right away I found a clipping

Melinda's U. of Pittsburgh MBA
Melinda & Michael Spring,
Patrick & Jonathan

from the Sonoma Index-Tribune, which discussed "The poison of resentment." It was written by Joanne Braun of the Sonoma Shambhala Meditation Center. She quotes the Buddhist teacher Pema Chodron who observed that "Resentment is like drinking rat poison, and hoping the other person will die." She goes on to say that resentment causes suffering, not to the object of our anger, but to ourselves.

Ms. Braun believes that we have tremendous power to affect our own peace of mind, and have the power to let the resentment go, and perhaps even understand the humanity and perspective of the other party. I'm ready to try again to let the resentment go, and will start by trying to show appreciation and gratitude every day. I'll ponder the question while I write more about 1990 and 1991.

There were many significant blessings that deserve my gratitude. In 1990 Melinda received her M.B.A. after she had used the maximum number of postponements while she gave birth to two babies 16 months apart. The little boys gazed wide-eyed at their mother in her cap and gown.

Michael was proud and happy at his wife's achievement.

Melinda and Michael liked their old Victorian house, but knew the school system there wasn't good and were thinking ahead. They found a larger home in an outstanding school district where Jonathan started kindergarten in a few years.

We continued to enjoy living in Pittsburgh. Our visitors especially liked going to the wave pool. I liked my quilting, DAR, and church activities. Quilt shows were sometimes in unusual places such as the Phipps Conservatory or a turn-of-the-century mansion. I never tired of looking at the intricate needlework and learning how to do some myself. In those years we were guests at two weddings that allowed me to wear my dressy, but not too dressy, mother-of-the-bride outfit again.

Dinah decided to move to Seattle. She found that she needed at least three things in her life: a job, a place to live, and a relationship. After eight-and-a-half years in New York City she hadn't been able to find more than two out of three.

Alison and Chuck were moving to Frederick, Maryland, where Chuck was working. Dan, who now had some disposable income, bought his first car, a black sports model. Happy is an inadequate word to describe how he felt about having his first real car.

Art's Office

Events were happening so fast that it was hard to keep up with everything. Art was in the countdown to retirement with all its financial and life-changing adjustments. We were available to go anywhere anytime, as long as money and energy held out. One of the first things we did was visit Alison and Chuck in their new home, a lovely place to welcome their new baby in December.

In May 1991 we decided to visit California again. Melvin still lived and worked in Livermore, but also had bought a retirement home in Oakmont. He picked us up at the airport and took us to his new house. We were still on cordial terms, and he let us use his car while we were in California. We drove to Seattle to see Dinah's new location.

We hadn't been to that city before and it was exciting to explore its wonders. Dinah was happy with her job there, and also happy that she had met a man, Steve Havas, the first week in Seattle. A friend introduced them in a store parking lot and they saw each other every day thereafter.

We traveled up and down the coast, visiting both scenic sites and Art's relatives. Dad Coops and Cathryn were settled in the Sonoma condo. Settled is perhaps the wrong word. Dad Coops missed his Kenwood house and Cathryn wasn't happy with life anymore. She had thought that when she was in Sonoma it would be easier to go to the things that she enjoyed there. That was true for about six months and then she became almost reclusive and increasingly distraught.

Cathryn didn't go with us when we took Dad Coops to the Sonoma Coast. We stopped at the Kenwood house where we talked to Gabriel, the Mexican caretaker, who had lived in the nearby cottage for many years. Gabriel was very fond of Dad Coops and almost part of the family. It was obvious that Gabriel and Dad Coops agreed that living in the house there would be better than in the condo.

Back in Pittsburgh, the summer passed happily with visits from my brother and sister and families, and getting together with friends. Alison and Chuck were about five hours away in Frederick, and we decided to go there in September. Alison was postponing her career for now as they prepared for their first child.

Amy Ruhl & Dan Coops
Oct. 1991
Wedding Site, Peekskill, NY

Leaf-peeping is an annual activity in the fall, and we combined that with visiting Dan and Amy in Ossining, New York. Nearby was a huge reservoir that I found fascinating. It was part of the water supply for N.Y.C., which made me a bit concerned for the people of that city. The reservoir had been built by the W.P.A. during the 1930s. However, the craftsmanship was beautiful, and apparently still doing its job very well. This area of New York had seen much history being made. Washington Irving lived and wrote there. Signs mentioned Sleepy Hollow, and we toured the Old Dutch Cemetery, founded in 1687, where Irving is buried.

Dan and Amy were planning to make some history of their own in Peekskill. They took us to the site near the Hudson River where they were to be married the following June. They planned to have an outdoor ceremony near Monte Verde, a large and imposing building where the reception would be held.

Grandma Shirley & baby Jessica Feb. 1992

Soon the holiday season was upon us, and it was an even busier time than usual. A good friend, Barbara Rogers, with whom I had shared many car-pool jobs, invited us to their oldest daughter's wedding. It was held in the imposing Gothic-style Presbyterian Church where we had belonged for many years before moving to Pittsburgh. Barbara was a natural born hostess and the wedding was a beautiful affair. The lovely bride and two equally attractive sisters made the scene perfect.

Melinda, Michael and the boys, and also Dan and Amy, came for Thanksgiving. It's hard to believe now that I put together so many big meals. But the time had come when we also shared meals at their homes where they did the cooking.

"It's a girl!" was the news on December 3 when our first grand-daughter arrived. Jessica was a big healthy baby and Alison was glad the difficult delivery was over. The baby was perfect and our visit to see her was well documented. Dinah traveled to Pittsburgh from Seattle for Christmas. We all went to Melinda and Michael's house, and then on another day they came to ours. Somehow we all went to Frederick to see Alison, Chuck, and the new Jessica. Dan and Amy came, too. The family added up to a dozen people now.

We heard that the situation in California wasn't so happy. In Mel-

104

vin's Christmas letter he said that Cathryn had been complaining of intense back pain and the doctor had put her in the hospital. Dad Coops needed someone with him and had 24-hour care. Things were "turbulent at best." Melvin said that a nursing home for both Dad Coops and Cathryn was a definite option, and he was very busy "covering all bases."

Bill Morris and his wife, Verna, were deeply involved in the whole problem. Bill was Dad Coops' step-son by his late wife, Esther Morris, and he had continued to help the family. He found himself taking care of the book work and many other duties connected with Dad and Cathryn's care, and didn't think it was his place to do these things. We were soon to hear much more about that.

FLYING INTO THE EYE OF THE STORM

It was Art's first full year of retirement, and we were launched into the world of Social Security and Medicare. Art never suffered any trauma in the transition. After 43 years of going to work he was content to be at home. We hadn't planned anything in particular but things just started happening.

We had never been concerned about Art's brother Melvin having Power of Attorney for their father and being executor of his will because we believed he would do a conscientious and efficient job. But as time went by and conditions changed, so did his agenda. As that fountain of wisdom, Ann Landers, once quoted, "If you want to know the true character of a person, share an inheritance with him."

Melvin made it plain that he didn't need any help. He said he had never worked on a committee and didn't intend to start now. Committee? Wasn't it a family? He said he didn't want Art to "muck things up." Muck what up? We had a copy of the will and it seemed straightforward. Esther had asked Dad Coops to remember her three sons and he had included a percentage for them. Esther Morris had been married to Dad Coops for 17 years. She used her own money to help keep the ranch going, and deserved a share of the estate. Dad Coops also made provision for his wife Cathryn's care, and the remainder was to be divided among Art, Melvin, and Betty, except that Melvin was to get the farm machinery and the pickup truck.

Melvin told Art that a percentage of the estate was too generous for the Morris sons, and he had convinced his father to change it to a dollar amount, a move that turned out to be illegal because there had been a written agreement specifying the terms.

Information concerning Melvin and the estate came out gradually over a period of time, and my journal in the first few months of 1992 only shows much agitation as we tried to digest new information. Melvin would call one time and be livid, and then another time be nice as pie. Mid-January, he said that he, along with Bill and Verna Morris, had moved

Dad Coops back to Kenwood and had hired full-time care, while Cathryn moved into a nursing home in Sonoma. Bill Morris was one of Esther's sons and Dad Coops' stepson. Bill and his wife Verna were very helpful in assisting Dad and Cathryn.

The relationship with Melvin became ever more prickly, and he and Art weren't able to have a productive conversation. It was impossible to work with Melvin. We talked to Bill and Verna Morris and also to Dad Coops' care-givers. It was a worrisome picture. February didn't bring any answers, and in March we decided to go and see for ourselves. We felt like making it a real vacation by driving across the country, and we had a wonderful time. Art's favorite kind of vacation was to drive and see the country. At the Alamo we heard a presidential candidate, Paul Tsongas.

Art and his father in Sonoma
Art Irving Coops and Arthur Coops

A lady sitting next to me said she was from Arkansas and was going to vote for Bill Clinton. I didn't think many people would do that.

It was good to see Art's sister and family when we arrived in Arizona, and in another couple of days we were in Kenwood. We were glad to see Dad Coops back in his own home. I cooked quite a few dinners for visitors. Art's cousins, his nephew and family, Bill and Verna, and even Melvin came once. Dad Coops was glad to be back in Kenwood, but he missed Cathryn terribly.

We drove to Seattle where Dinah and Steve were living in a nice apartment with a view across a lake and to the mountains. Seattle seemed to be agreeing with Dinah just fine. Instead of heading home, we decided to go back to Kenwood because we were so uneasy about the situation there. Melvin was disgusted to see us again and said, "It would have been shorter if you had gone straight back to Pittsburgh." He said when we were in Kenwood it messed up his agreements with Dad's care-givers. He was still living and working in Livermore but

107

came to his Oakmont retirement home on weekends.

Bill and Verna Morris invited us for dinner. They had been in the eye of the storm for quite a while and would be happy for Art to help. Art had some authority while Bill didn't. Dad Coops liked to go to the coast, so one day we drove there again. Along the way he said, "Why don't you close the door on your house and come live with me?" That was a big consideration to think about as we drove back to Pennsylvania.

Dan Coops and Amy Ruhl Wedding
June 13, 1992

Dan and Amy's wedding was in a couple of months and we were thinking about that, too. At some point Art's sister, Betty, called and said that Melvin told her that unless she or Art had another idea, he was moving Dad Coops into a nursing home. Home care was too expensive. Now Melvin was worried that the dollar amount that the Morrises would get could be greater than the Coops numbers. His carefully laid plans were in trouble.

Betty wondered if we would be able to come and help. Then Art's cousins in Lompoc called. Marguerite said that we would never be sorry if we came and helped Dad Coops. She still regretted that they hadn't come to look after Uncle Harry, Dad Coops' brother. We started to plan a temporary move and tried to foresee some of the complications. I was ready to give it serious consideration, not only because Dad Coops needed us, but I'll admit that I was finding Art's retirement quite boring and thought a change of scene would be good, especially in Sonoma Valley.

But first there was the wedding. Marguerite said that Dan and Amy had invited them and they would like to come. They planned to take the train across the country to Pittsburgh, and then go to the wedding with us. That sounded like such fun and we were very pleased with their decision. When we met them at the train station they said they were glad they had done it, but didn't want to do it again.

The day before the wedding we drove to Sleepy Hollow country, and saw more of the fascinating sights there. Harry and Marguerite were impressed with the history represented in the area. We had an excellent docent who gave us many details as we toured Washington Irving's home, "Sunnyside."

At the rehearsal dinner we met Amy's family for the first time: her parents, sister, and two brothers. It was a nice dinner with their family, Melinda, Michael and their little boys, and Harry and Marguerite. The day of the wedding Dinah and Steve arrived from Seattle, and Alison, Chuck, and baby Jessica from Maryland.

I had been with Amy the year before when she made her choices of flowers for the wedding. She was quite specific in what she wanted and they did look lovely. The weather cooperated and the scene was perfect with a background of the Hudson River and the mountains, and the lawn set with white chairs for guests and an arbor for the bridal party. The guests arrived, except for one of Dan's friends who had set his alarm for p.m. instead of a.m. He was late, but everybody else was assembled to watch as Dan and Amy exchanged vows. It was in Peekskill, New York on June 13, 1992.

Food and dancing followed and it was quite a festive occasion. Marguerite loves weddings and always looks as happy as the bride. Many pictures document the occasion. My pink mother-of-the-bride dress made its final appearance.

We had another couple of days with Harry and Marguerite in Pittsburgh before taking them to the airport for their flight home. Marguerite was an expert quilter and quilting teacher, and she especially enjoyed visiting Amish country and seeing their quilts. Now we had to concentrate on packing for California. We were told that it was unlikely that Dad Coops would live more than six months. He would be ninety-seven in November.

GAS AND OIL OKAY ?

It was hard to decide what to pack in the boxes we were having sent to California. I'd never been in California during the winter. Saying long goodbyes to Melinda and family and then to Alison was hard. The grandchildren were so adorable. Our next door neighbor promised to keep an eye on our house, and Melinda said she would come occasionally and check on our cars.

Art felt he should take an active role in taking care of his father, so on July 25, 1992, we boarded a jumbo jet headed for San Francisco. I'd never been on such a big plane, and sitting in the middle of the middle felt like being in an auditorium. I had a strange detached feeling of unreality.

We arrived in Kenwood, and Melvin said, "I see you're here, not that anybody invited you." He meant that he hadn't invited us. Apparently his father, sister, cousins, and the Morrises who had invited us didn't count. He handed Art a pile of paperwork concerning the hired caretakers and the necessary legal forms for having employees. We would still need their help occasionally.

To show Art how much work he had been doing Melvin also gave Art a large box full of monthly and annual reports of companies in which Dad owned stock. He said he'd been burdened with a lot of responsibility. After Melvin left Art looked at the top envelope and I'll never forget the look on his face. He was stunned. Somehow Melvin had added his name and changed the stock investments into JTWROS, "Joint Tenant with Right of Survivorship." That meant that when their father died, those investments would go directly to Melvin without being included in the estate. Did Melvin think that Art had no idea what the new designation meant? Art asked a lawyer friend what should be done about JTWROS, and was told, "You must get that changed before your father dies, or nothing can be done." Dad Coops was now 96 years of age.

Other than trying to cope with Melvin, it was surprisingly easy to settle into the routine. Dad Coops didn't need nursing care, which we would have been unable to supply. I shopped and cooked and Art did outside work, which is what he liked to do anywhere. I'd always loved the big old house, but never expected to be able to live there. After about a week, I was sitting upstairs in the sunroom and looking out at the mountains and the surrounding landscape and thought, "I love it here!" Right now it didn't look like the minefield it was. Before talking about more explosions I'd like to take a break to tell about our job in Kenwood.

Caretaking comes in many forms but in most cases it requires 24/7 attention. Dad Coops' care was easy in many ways. He could take care of his own personal needs and get around without assistance. He even went up and down the long flight of steps. His collection of canes went unused because he refused to use any of them.

We found that he liked to go for rides, and sometimes we went to the Napa Valley. As we approached Yountville and the Veterans' Hospital he always said, "That's where I had my appendix out." At St. Helena it was "I went with Ma to visit Aunt Yenny here." At Calistoga we would stop for ice cream.

Every ride in the car was preceded by, "Gas and oil okay? That was always my job." Sometimes the question came before we were in the car, and sometimes not until after we were on our way. We assured him that we had run out of gas only once and that had been in about 1950, and Art was conscientious about changing oil every 3000 miles.

Our road trips continued uneventfully. Dad enjoyed going to the coast and sitting by the ocean. Art and I would go for walks on the beach, but always kept his hat in sight. He became confused if we went to visit relatives in the Bay Area and kept asking where we were going. He forgot there was the San Rafael-Richmond Bridge, so trips going in that direction were troublesome to him. He was reassured when we kept telling him who we would visit.

We called on his old friends in Sonoma, too. He had a good visit with Al Stornetta, and another day we went to Mary Bundschu's house. Dad and Mary's husband had gone to fruit growers' meetings together. We also stopped in to see former employees, Matilda and Kenny Roeder. Kenny had been a box maker and Matilda was a fruit packer during Dad's ranching days.

Dad's late wife, Esther, was from a large family, which embraced all newcomers with equal affection. They accepted Cathryn and they also welcomed all of us who were in Dad Coops' family. Occasionally his large wrap-round porch held 30 people in a family get-together.

On Sundays we attended the Sonoma United Methodist Church. I had been a Presbyterian since my parents took me to church as an infant and enrolled me in the Cradle Roll Department. But people at the Methodist Church knew Dad Coops, and his wife Cathryn had been quite active in the women's groups.

On Veterans Day we went to the V.F.W. observance. Dad Coops had served as commander of Post 1943 more than once through the years.

Thursday was "Lunch Bunch" day. Fred Nilson, Hudson Auberlin, Louie Minelli, and sometimes other gentlemen were in the congenial group. Louie's wife, Helene, was often there. Art had known Louie Minelli for years because Louie had hauled Coops fruit to San Francisco and on the way back to Sonoma he had brought produce for various local grocery stores.

Cathryn had enjoyed joining in the Lunch Bunch fun, but now we only saw her in the nursing home when we visited about every other day. She was always in bed and would flinch when Dad Coops touched her. She said her back hurt and it was very painful. Cathryn had no debilitating disease but said she was tired of living and wanted to die. She said her life had been wonderful and she had no complaints at all but enough was enough. She had been a lady of many talents and losing her would be very sad. She was 86.

Dad Coops missed having Cathryn home with him but had forgotten much about the years of their marriage. His short-term memory was gone but we still often heard about when he was in France during WWI. He had the gift of remembering good parts of his life and forgetting the bad things, except for his rage against Bank of America. He blamed the bank for unjustly foreclosing on him and forcing him off his property in 1938.

It was obvious that he suffered from dementia. It wasn't Alzheimer's. He had no tendency whatever to wander away. He kept thinking that all he needed to improve his eyesight was a good doctor. Even the best doctors said that macular degeneration had taken his center vision. He had always loved to read so losing that ability was sorrowful. I found a number of magnifying glasses here and there. He was sure something would help him see well. His hearing loss was also a handicap.

A highlight of every day was going to the post office. The United States Postal Service had no fan more devoted than Dad Coops. The post office was a short walk from his house and he was always eager to go. He would usually sit on a log along the way for a short rest before reaching his destination and opening his box. Somebody had put a little "smiley face" on his P.O. Box.

Art's sister loved her father dearly and called every week. During their conversations we would hear him say, "I'm just too old." Dad Coops was very undemanding. He never asked us for anything or to do anything. Bath time was the worst night of the week and it took a lot of persuasion. While Art helped him I would take away his dirty clothes and put his Sunday outfit on his "dressing chair." On other nights getting hold of his dirty clothes was a problem. I started to listen for when he got up at night, and then I would whisk away his underwear and socks and replace them with clean ones. He didn't want his clothes washed very often because that "would wear them out."

If we heard the question, "What goes on here?" we knew he was upset about something. He could still hear and see well enough to know when something out of the ordinary was happening. Once Bill and Verna were upstairs helping to move some furniture for us and Dad Coops heard it and became quite agitated. Art knew it wouldn't be a good idea to try to do anything about termites and dry rot at that time.

Choosing Dad's outfits was easy because he only wore khaki shirts and pants except on Sundays. I wrote down where he kept things: his pencils and notebook in his shirt pocket, keys in his right pants pocket, and handkerchief and wallet in his back pockets. I forget what was in the left pocket, but it was important, too.

He could be so funny. One Sunday morning at breakfast he looked down at his pants and said, "Hmm, must be Sunday." He ate almost anything but didn't like garlic or herbs, pronounced with the "h." At his next checkup the doctor was glad to see that Dad had gained eight pounds. If the doctor had my record he would have known I had gained, too. Perhaps my zeal for fixing good food was excessive.

Dad and Cathryn hadn't used the sun porch, and at one point it was a cluttered-up storage space. But it had been cleaned out, and I liked to sit there. I usually left the door open, and when Dad Coops went by he would always close it. Once I said, "I like that little room. It's my..." but I couldn't think of a word. He said, "Retreat?" Exactly right. Sometimes I very much needed a shelter from the storm.

GET A LAWYER!

If I could have weather custom made I would want it like the Sonoma Valley. It was late summer in 1992 and I marveled at the glorious days of sunshine and harvest. A former caretaker, Ruby Stewart, who was a family friend, stopped in and said she could help when we needed her. She asked if Melvin was releasing enough money for Dad's care. I said yes, we had opened a checking account and he put money in it. She said, "He's giving you a lollipop because he doesn't want you to find the candy store." That was a curious remark.

When I went to the bank to withdraw some money the teller hesitated, said to please wait a minute, and disappeared. She came back and said the account was overdrawn. Melvin had reduced the amount without telling us. Art had asked him to get his name off their father's stocks and he angrily refused. Melvin said that if Art didn't stop meddling he and his brokerage would see to it that he lost his home, cars, investments—everything he had. He even pulled a list of his threats out of his pocket so he wouldn't forget anything. Art almost laughed because it was so ridiculous.

However, when Melvin called their sister and told her all the bad things he would do to us she was scared. Betty called and her voice was shaky and weak. Art told her not to worry because it was all hot air, and she continued to support us. However, Art did call his own broker who advised him to get in touch with the head of the San Francisco brokerage. When Art explained the problems they froze Melvin's accounts because they didn't want to be involved in a lawsuit.

The trouble escalated. Melvin had tried to obtain Cathryn's Power of Attorney, too, but she said absolutely not. She said she didn't trust Melvin "as far as she could throw a grand piano." She said he was "grabby" and she thought some hanky-panky was going on. We took it seriously because Cathryn was still very sharp.

Melvin went on a business trip and when he came back he acted quite friendly. I said it was the power of prayer but Art said he either had an ulterior motive or was on medication. Art thought it would be wise to consult an attorney so after some inquiries we got a grandpa-sitter and kept our appointment with Charles Harris in Sonoma. We had been in California less than a month and were into a situation that was completely beyond anything we had experienced in 40 years of marriage and raising four children. It was a different world.

After investigation, Mr. Harris advised Art to get Dad's Power of Attorney and be the executor of the will. Since Cathryn favored that idea, the lawyer was willing to go to the nursing home. He explained to Dad what was happening and his advice about the P.O.A. Dad Coops kept saying, "Melvin has plenty of money already. He doesn't need mine." But when he asked Cathryn if he was doing the right thing to give Art the P.O.A. and change executors, she said, "Yes, dear, you are." He added a codicil to his will making Art his executor. His signatures were notarized.

Dad Coops and Shirley 1992

Without Cathryn's support it would have been impossible. Dad Coops trusted her implicitly. Art and the lawyer thought it could all be settled in a couple of weeks. I said, "God willing" and Cathryn added "and the devil doesn't mind."

Apparently the devil did mind because Melvin hired a lawyer and said he would take Art to court. The two lawyers were good negotiators and worked out a compromise, which would give the brothers equal responsibility. First Melvin agreed but then kept backing away. One of his conditions was that Art give the P.O.A. back to him exclusively.

It was one thing after another. Now Melvin was saying that Cathryn had enough money to pay for her own care in the nursing home, especially since she had stolen stock from Dad Coops. That was ridiculous. For her birthdays and their anniversary Cathryn always said she wanted stock. To her, nothing said love like P.G. & E. stock, so that stock was definitely hers. She also had an inheritance from her Aunt Lizzie and money from her first marriage when her husband ran a pharmacy. She had no children and had earned her own money for years. She and Dad kept their assets separate and she was leaving hers to her brother and sisters.

The fall rains arrived and the legal dueling continued. Looking after Dad Coops was a cinch compared to coping with Melvin. Dad had his 97th birthday in November. I had a little dinner a couple of days before and invited Art's cousin and his wife and Melvin. Melvin didn't reply but did appear as we were passing the food so I set another place. Step-brother Bill Morris and his wife Verna invited us to their house for dinner on Dad's birthday. Bill and Verna were solid rocks of support for us.

The following weekend Dad Coops' family by his late wife, Esther, arrived. There were Morrises by the dozen and about 30 people came to help celebrate Dad's birthday. They brought lots of food, including a birthday cake that was an artistic creation baked by one of the women who ran a bakery.

The presidential election was held in November 1992 and we sent our absentee ballots to Pennsylvania. Art voted for Clinton and I was one of the 19 million voting for Perot, which helped seal the fate of George H.W. Bush. William Jefferson Clinton was inaugurated in January.

The holidays were just around the corner. Dinah and Steve came from Seattle to spend Thanksgiving with us. In early December Alison and one-year-old Jessica came to visit. Jessica had walked at 9 months so it was such fun to have the patter of little feet around the house. At Christmas time we got a tree and I found ornaments in the basement. Bill and Verna invited us for a festive Christmas dinner at their house in Santa Rosa.

We received many photos of our grandchildren as they played in the snow. It was rain here, torrents of it. I'd never seen anything like California in January. Then in February glorious springtime started with the lovely camellias.

Dad Coops' health continued to be good considering his age. He had occasional coughs and once in a while a backache. One night we heard a crash in his bedroom and found that he had fallen and cut his lip on the foot of his bed. It bled profusely, but eventually stopped and he went to sleep just fine. He had no ill effects except for a fat lip. The next

117

day the dentist said his teeth were okay.

One day I was driving Dad to Sonoma to see Cathryn and the engine warning light came on. I should have kept quiet but I reflexively said, "The engine light was on for a second." Dad Coops said, "What? Somebody should have checked the gas and oil at home. That was always my job!" But we got home just fine and Art took the car to the garage. Gas and oil were okay, but the water pump wasn't. Another little crisis was averted.

Dad Coops still enjoyed rides in the car, if the gas and oil were okay. He did get disgusted when he saw yet another vineyard being planted. He would grumble, "More grapes." He had liked to grow cherries, pears, apples, figs, prunes, and walnuts. He'd had a big dehydrator on Eighth Street East in Sonoma for drying fruit. If he had fancied grapes and planted a vineyard on his 40+ acre Kenwood ranch, the family history would likely have been quite different.

Life was normal around the Kenwood house. Mexican caretaker and good friend, Gabriel, who helped with outdoor work, and his family lived in the cottage. He had a flock of chickens that pecked around the place all day. I told Cathryn I liked to watch the chickens and she said I was hard up for entertainment. Any diversion from the Melvin agony was welcome. Melvin should have been a lawyer because he was always wanting to go to court. Our lawyer decided the only solution was for Art to file for his father's conservatorship. The petition for this expensive process was presented to the court, and a hearing scheduled for March 16, 1993.

Getting a conservatorship was a complicated and exacting process. A court investigator came to the house to assess the situation. Dad Coops was always gracious to visitors, and he answered her questions to the best of his ability. The investigator had already questioned Art extensively. She was ready to make her report to the judge.

We had support at the conservatorship hearing from the lawyers: ours, Dad Coops', Cathryn's, and also a number of friends. Melvin's lawyer was there alone without his client, which was strange because we were finally in court. He may have thought it was just a routine motion and the judge would postpone a decision. But instead, the petition was granted and the judge ordered all Dad's assets into a temporary conservatorship until the final hearing. The Court Investigator's report had tipped the balance. She said that granting Art the conservatorship would be in his father's best interest. Melvin fired his lawyer.

1993 THINGS SETTLE DOWN, SORT OF

We had strong ties on both sides of the country. After respite breaks at our own house in Pittsburgh I both anticipated and dreaded going back to California. But we always resumed our routine there as though we hadn't been away. After our April 1993 trip it was intensely satisfying to start getting all the accounting information ready to take to the court-approved accountant who required to-the-penny numbers. We were relieved to know that Dad's finances would be under court scrutiny. Melvin had kept $10,000 for "services rendered" but was told that should go in the pot, too. The lawyer said to sell the stocks because they would be too hard to divide, so that solved the problem of Melvin's name JT-WROS on them.

We had to reorganize quickly because Dinah and Steve's Seattle wedding was to be in two weeks, May 8, 1993. Our four children's wed-

dings were all quite different. One was in a hotel, another in a church, and the third was outdoors with views of the river and mountains.

This time we were invited to a Seattle park for a casual venue. My mother-of-the-bride dress wouldn't do. The men were told that neckties weren't necessary but I suspected that umbrellas would be. My umbrella was purple, and my dress a longish black-and-white print. Dinah said I looked like Mary Poppins.

The wedding day started out sunny. Dan and Amy had arrived from Vermont and we all stayed at a bed and breakfast. The morning of

Dinah and Steve
Seattle Wedding, May 8, 1993

the wedding the four of us went to the Space Needle and various other sites. As the ceremony hour drew near so did some dark clouds coming over the mountain. Vows were said with the official, the bride, groom, and guests standing close together in the park shelter. The sun was shining again for the reception on the patio of Dinah and Steve's apartment.

Meanwhile, back at the California ranch, life went on as before. Art had the opportunity to do as much gardening as he wished. We still visited Cathryn every other day, and took Dad Coops on rides through the Napa Valley or to Goat Rock on the Sonoma coast. Dad's health was

Four Generations July 1993
Art Irving Coops, Jonathan Spring, Arthur A. Coops,
Patrick Spring, Melinda Coops Spring

about the same although he was getting weaker physically and mentally. He was undemanding and cooperative, except for baths. The most difficult part of care-giving was his same questions over and over. We could only talk about long ago happenings and people. He couldn't retain current events. But we had our own space in the big house and we had frequent visits from friends and family.

July brought a change in routine when daughter Melinda and her husband, Michael, drove our car across the country. Jon and Pat were small but good little travelers. Over at the coast Melinda's husband took pictures of the four generations. He also made a video of his interview with Dad Coops. We went to various other local sites. A special treat was visiting the house near Sonoma where Art had grown up. The people who lived there graciously showed us around. Dad Coops went everywhere with us except to Marine World.

Our next respite break was in September. Arriving back in Kenwood after the long plane ride from Pittsburgh I wasn't happy to see Melvin's car in the driveway. I hadn't seen him for nearly a year. Art talked to him while I stayed in the kitchen and broke out in red splotches. Melvin was returning money from a dividend check that Art had tracked down. It had been sent to Melvin's address and he had put the money in his own account. The lawyer said no, that goes in the pot, too.

In October two of our daughters got together when Alison, with little Jessica, visited Dinah in Seattle so we flew to Seattle to be with them. Our family was scattered but we managed to make contact occasionally. I hoped I could remember which direction we were flying and why.

We observed Dad Coops' ninety-eighth birthday on November 4. Stepbrothers Bill and Jack Morris and their wives came for the birthday dinner, which was complete with a traditional cake for dessert. Dad's sweet tooth was still intact.

Dad Coops' 98th Birthday

The remaining days of 1993 were routine, except for November 8, when I found that we were located near the Rodgers Creek fault. When I heard the loud noise I knew what it was, even though I had never experienced an earthquake before. The quake registered 3.5. We were sitting at the kitchen table and Dad's peripheral vision allowed him to see the books moving on top of the refrigerator. There's nothing to like about an earthquake. I felt somewhat disoriented.

November continued with Veterans Day at the V.F.W. where they were celebrating the organization's 75th anniversary. Dad Coops was honored for being a 60 year member. We spent both Thanksgiving and Christmas with Bill and Verna Morris. They helped us through many difficult times. I called Verna my therapist.

122

Just before New Year we got a grandpa-sitter and went to Stinson Beach. It was a lovely day and we ate lunch outside. The waitress said there had been frost there in the morning. What a remarkable climate! I thought I was ready to face 1994.

◄◄ | ►►

1994 DEATH DID THEM PART

Our expected six months of caretaking had stretched to a year and a half. Dad Coops, now 98 years of age, was still able to take care of his own needs, go up and down the long stairway, and eat and sleep well. The most difficult part for me was the constant questions and trying to help him make sense of news stories that he heard on TV. The O.J. Simpson matter was especially challenging.

When Dad heard about the earthquake in southern California he didn't quite believe it. To him there was only the "Big One" in 1906. He had never heard of southern California earthquakes. But then he wondered if his "adopted" sister Tinka, in Bakersfield, was all right (Tinka was no longer living). But our routines were basically the same and things were as normal as they ever were.

It was sad for us all to see Cathryn failing. Dad couldn't believe that she could no longer talk or feed herself and sometimes didn't seem to recognize us. We had made plans for an April trip east because we needed a break and also should check on our Pittsburgh house and our family around there. Capable people would look after Dad and Cathryn. We flew to Pittsburgh on April 12, the day that daughter Alison gave birth to their second child. We liked being in our own house while taking side trips to see friends and relatives. One trip was to Frederick, Maryland, to see new baby Andrew, our fourth grandchild.

We had been in Pittsburgh about ten days when we received word that Cathryn had had a severe stroke. She died a few days later, on April 22, 1994, at age 87. Stepbrother and good friend Bill Morris assured us that he could take care of arrangements. Bill was Dad Coops' second wife's son and Dad's third wife's executor. Cathryn had asked that her body be shipped back to Michigan for burial and Bill followed her wishes. After more family consultations we decided to keep to our plan for returning to California the end of April and then have Cathryn's memorial service in May.

The hired caretakers appeared to be thrilled to see us back and to be done with their jobs. Dad was confused about Cathryn. Sometimes he thought that she had decided to leave him and return to Michigan. The memorial service was on May 13 and it may have helped him understand, at least for the moment, that she had died.

Cathryn had chosen the music and scriptures for her service. Many friends and relatives gathered in the Methodist Church to remember her. We enjoyed meeting her delightful family: sister, brother, and nieces. People spoke of her being always the gracious hostess with groups large and small. Her interests were varied; avid reader, sports fan, card shark, astute collector, and student of American history. She had said herself that her life had been wonderful and she had no complaints.

Cathryn's executor, Bill Morris, and his wife Verna, sorted her belongings, with some things to sell and many others that were to be sent to her relatives. Cathryn also had beautiful furniture, which would be left in place for the time being.

I spent hours at my new word processor. Art had decided to write about his family's history because now he had time and he was in the right environment. Many typed pages resulted. Besides my personal letters, I was also typing documents for the accountant. We went to her house several times so she could instruct us and clarify what was needed for court-approved financial reporting for a conservatorship. Eventually it was finished, submitted, and copies sent to Betty and Melvin.

For the first time Art had an opportunity to go to a Sonoma High School class reunion, Class of 1944, which happened to be their 50th. Two cousins had also graduated in that class and they came and stayed overnight with us. Dad Coops didn't understand what that was about and was confused and upset. Anything out of the ordinary troubled him.

Our second anniversary of living in California came and went. One Thursday I decided to invite Dad's "Lunch Bunch" to come to our house instead of going to the usual restaurant. Dad thought this rather strange, but he knew these people well. After lunch we sat out on the porch and had a nice visit. Dad Coops had four more days to live.

August 1st was a typical day. We went to Sonoma (gas and oil okay?) and did some errands. Then we stopped at McDonalds for hamburgers. Dad Coops had always been a big hamburger fan, and I liked to go to McDonalds so I could see some children.

That evening Dad ate a normal dinner, which that day included a favorite side dish, a bowl of rice with milk and sugar. A lady called and said she would like to talk to Dad Coops about his WWI experiences because she was writing an article about WWI. We made an appointment for the next morning. Dad climbed the stairs and prepared for bed as usual.

A4 – Friday, August 5, 1994   The Sonoma Index-Tribune

OBITUARIES

Arthur Coops, member of pioneer ranching family here, dies at 98

Arthur August Coops, whose parents were pioneer ranchers of Sonoma Valley nearly a century ago, and who, himself, became one of the best-known agriculturists in the county from the 1920s through the 1950s, died on Tuesday, Aug. 2, 1994, at his residence in Kenwood.

Born near Sebastopol on Nov. 4, 1895, he was 98.

He was only a year old when his family moved to Sonoma Valley, settling on what is today the Stornetta ranch, adjacent to the Napa County line, living in a house rented from family members with whom his father was engaged in ranching.

Mr. Coops attended the original Huichica one-room elementary school at Vineburg, and later the Lick-Wilmerding high school in San Francisco with his older brother, the late Harry Coops. Meanwhile, their father, J. H. Coops, purchased two ranches off Napa Road, the seven-acre Ellis place, and then the 356-acre Proletti ranch with its 100 acres of tillable land, establishing the family as prominent fruit growers.

Arthur Coops, known to his many friends as "Art," served in France during World War I. After his discharge he returned to California and joined his father and Harry, in their fruit-growing, packing and drying enterprises, which involved four local ranches, two on Napa Road and two in Buena Vista. Although the ranches were lost late in the Depression era, Mr. Coops later repurchased the Eighth Street East packing plant and dehydration business and re-established himself.

From this site he also operated a Rockgas propane-distributing business, building it from 19 customers in 1940 to 1,700 customers in 1956 when he sold the business and purchased the Greene ranch in Kenwood where he resided until his death on Tuesday.

During his tenure in Sonoma Valley he served for 18 years on the Cherry Growers Association board, 35 years on the Prune Board and seven years on the Pear Growers Association board. He was a past director of the Sonoma County Water Conservation Board and was a founding member of Bear Flag Post, Veterans of Foreign Wars.

In 1921, Mr. Coops married the late Aloha Millard and they had three children, all of whom survive him – Betty James of Sumerton, Ariz.; Irving Coops of Kenwood and Melvin Coops of Santa Rosa. Three stepsons, from his marriage to Esther Morris in 1956, also survive him – Jack Morris, Vacaville; Bill Morris, Santa Rosa and Jim Morris, Los Molinas. After Esther's death in 1972, Mr. Coops married Cathryn Vallier, who died April 22, 1994, in a local convalescent hospital.

Other survivors of Mr. Coops include six grandchildren, 10 step-grandchildren, seven great-grandchildren, 15 step-great-grandchildren and two step-great-great-grandchildren.

Funeral services will be held on Saturday, Aug. 6, at 2 p.m. at the Bates, Evans & Fehrensen funeral home in Sonoma, with viewing to begin at 10 a.m. that day.

Burial will be in Mountain Cemetery.

ARTHUR A. COOPS
Longtime Valley resident

The next morning I fixed his grapefruit, and then went to the basement to sort some dishes. About 9:00 I decided I'd better wake him so he could be ready for his interview. I knocked on his door, went in, and was struck by a strong, unpleasant odor. I touched his shoulder and got no response. Art was outside. I called to him and said, "Something's wrong!" Art saw no sign of life, so we called the doctor who said to call 9-1-1. They came quickly, but knew immediately they weren't needed. Gabriel, who lived in the cottage, had heard me call Art, and now he was slumped in a chair in the living room. We all knew there would be big changes in our lives.

1994 "NOBODY ELSE BETTER DIE!"

Young Reverend Mr. Ted Virts had been minister at the Sonoma United Methodist Church for only a month. He had already called on us and accepted an invitation to stay for supper so we became somewhat acquainted. The day after Dad Coops' death Rev. Virts came and spent an hour and a half with us. His remarks at the August 6 funeral were personal and touching. Dad had asked that the V.F.W. participate, and representatives were at the service and the cemetery. It was very hot and I'm sure they were uncomfortable. The gun salute was rather uneven; pop, pop—pop—pop, pop. However, they were wonderful old soldiers and we appreciated their being part of the ceremony.

The United Methodist Women arranged for the reception back at the church. As I was walking past the kitchen I heard somebody say, "Nobody else better die for a while!" I had to smile even though I sympathized. There had been a number of funerals in only a few months. I had often worked in church kitchens so was well aware of the time and effort required.

Fifteen people came back to the house after the funeral and shared a table full of food provided by friends. A few relatives stayed over that night. There was also an RV. Funerals are a mixture of sadness and pleasure. It was a joy to see so many friends and family, with one exception.

We hadn't seen Melvin for a year and a half but he came roaring back. He said to get all the papers together and the whole thing could be settled in a week or two. He wanted to sell the house immediately "as is" because there was "a can of worms under every rock." I couldn't believe he was talking about that wonderful old house. It was a Frank Lloyd Wright-inspired Prairie Style house built in 1915 and eligible for a Historic Landmark designation. Put it on the market now with the termites and dry rot and still needing to be cleaned out?

There wasn't a single point of agreement between the two brothers. They couldn't work together. Art was the executor and decided to go over or around Melvin and do what he thought needed to be done before putting the house on the market.

A couple of weeks after the funeral Art and I went to the Gravenstein Apple Fair. It felt like a breath of freedom the first time we went somewhere alone without either taking Dad Coops along or arranging for his care at home. It made me realize what a 24/7 job caretaking had been. But Melvin said that we were in California "ostensibly" to look after Dad Coops. He said we should start paying rent now. The lawyer was able to stave that off for a while. Meanwhile, Art was busy talking to realtors and contractors. They agreed that the porch roof wasn't safe and the inside of the house was sagging in the middle. Dry rot and termites had taken a toll.

Kenwood house repairs, February 1995

Months before Dad's death we had made plane reservations and arranged for his care while we went to Pennsylvania. We decided to go. We needed to check on our house and see friends and family. But soon it was time to leave Pittsburgh and go back "through the looking glass" to the California "wonderland."

We hadn't talked to Melvin directly. One day we were having lunch on Dad's back porch when Melvin drove in. My heart was pounding. I thought we could pull up a chair for him, put another plate on the table, and talk things over. But he didn't realize we were home from our trip and when he saw us he abruptly turned, jumped in his car, and sped off.

Contractors gave their assessments of the house damage and how much it would cost to fix it. This was difficult because Melvin was snapping at Art's heels and was very much against any repairs. In between

129

these confrontations and house duties we were able to do some fun things. We took a trip to the Gold Country and explored the area where Art's grandfather was born.

Dinah and Steve had made plans to come in early November to help celebrate Dad Coops' 99th birthday and we were so happy that they decided to come anyway. Soon it was Thanksgiving, which we observed in Arizona with Art's sister and family. It seemed certain that Holidays 1994 would be the last we would spend in Dad's house. We invited friends for Christmas dinner. For New Year's Eve we revived an old tradition. Bill and Verna Morris and a number of his cousins came for an evening of playing games and eating clam chowder. I fixed pork and sauerkraut for New Year's Day dinner. It would have been nice to have the holiday conviviality continue throughout the year.

However, January brought crashes and clashes. The contractor arrived with his two young helpers who seemed to enjoy their job of tearing off the porch. I stood at the front door and cried when the porch roof came crashing down. The rebuilding soon started and the lovely porch took shape again. The sturdy old porch floor was still fine.

The dry rot and termite damage were repaired and proper support built for the sagging floor of the house. Final repairs and inspections were completed by March and the house was put on the market. In April we escaped to the tranquility and normalcy of Pennsylvania for a short respite. Melvin was beside himself with anger because none of his plan was followed. The clashes were to continue for some time.

PART FIVE:
CALIFORNIA, HERE WE STAY

1995-1996 PLAN B

It soon became apparent that Dad Coops' house wasn't going to sell as a private residence. Traffic on Route 12 in 1995 was quite different than it had been in 1915. People who showed an interest in the property wanted to make it a "bed and breakfast." The location would be an asset to a business.

It was our job to make the house as attractive as possible to potential buyers. This was painful for me because I had been carrying on an illicit love affair with the old house, even though we were unsuited for each other. When people came to see the house my thought was "No, you can't have it!"

One interested party brought an architect, and another couple had a camera and a tape measure and checked everything. They said it was their dream house but I suspect they couldn't afford it. We, too, had to make a decision about where we would live. Art became more amenable to the idea of staying in California with its excellent gardening climate. But what could we afford that had enough land for his garden and orchard?

On Sundays we would scan the Open House ads and start out optimistically. If I liked a house Art might say, "There's nothing but rocks around it." If he saw some suitable land, I would probably say, "I hate this house." Usually both house and land were depressing. We were spoiled.

The realtor for Dad Coops' house had told us from the beginning that the three acres was large enough that it could be split. The sales agreement had two options. A price was listed for the whole property, and Plan B was a lesser price with one acre to stay with the estate. We didn't want a whole acre but that's how it was zoned.

However, nine months had gone by without an offer. Finally, in December a Kenwood couple offered a very low bid. The next week, Ray and Kathy Yahr from San Jose said they were interested. Competition was good news and the sale price looked better.

Kathy and Ray, with some sacrifice in the price of their San Jose house, sold it before the other folks sold theirs. We got to meet Kathy and Ray when they came to Kenwood with Kathy's parents, Frank and Marcia Mitchell. While Kathy and Ray talked to Art and the agent, I visited with Frank and Marcia. If the sale was a success they would live in the cottage while Kathy and Ray turned the main house into a bed and breakfast. They were agreeable to splitting the lot and letting us buy an acre from the estate.

During 1995 we took two trips back east and visited friends and family there. I knew that whichever place we lived I would miss the other place. But the momentum was moving towards us becoming California residents.

The crystal ball for 1996 was murky. I could see faint outlines of a new house for us but there were big black clouds hovering over it. Our old "Lunch Bunch" friend, Fred Nilson, said that if we told the County we wanted to build a house they would say, "We dare you." Melvin's reaction was, "I double-dare you." We had received a steady stream of objections from his lawyer. He kept threatening hearings and court trials. These seemed to be nuisance tactics that our lawyer was able to deflect.

We made some tentative steps to see if the plot could pass County requirements before going any further with our plans. A multitude of tests had to be passed, including one about getting clearance from several universities that there weren't any Indian artifacts on the property. Fortunately that one was waived. A house plan was taking shape. We asked the builder who had done the repairs on Dad's house if he would build a house for us and he said, "Sure."

We had joys and sorrows throughout the tumultuous year. Our good friend, Verna Morris, had routine bypass surgery in March but didn't survive. Then Bill and Verna's handicapped son died a few months later. Bill had many friends to help sustain him through these losses. He was very strong.

In early summer we prepared to leave Dad's house and move to an apartment at Fred Nilson's Loma Vista home near Sonoma. We traveled to Pittsburgh to put our house on the market and have our furniture sent to Santa Rosa for storage. Our house sold so quickly that we were able to complete almost all the arrangements before flying back to California. We moved out of two houses in July. I especially missed my sunroom retreat in Dad's house and I missed our pretty Pittsburgh house, too.

Before the year's end we had two new granddaughters, Tess in Seattle and Lauren in Frederick, Maryland. Son Dan and Amy had moved to Albuquerque from Vermont the previous November. Now Dan had decided to go back with IBM and they were returning to Burlington, Vermont. We did a lot of flying around as we went to see the new babies and Dan and Amy's new house.

Melvin wouldn't agree to anything. Now he said he wanted the acre and instructed his lawyer that no matter what Art bid he should bid $1000 more. He also wanted nearly $20,000 in rent for the year and a half we had lived there after Dad died and the house was repaired. What to do?

Art and new license plate

◀◀ | ▶▶

THIS OLD HOUSE

When I opened the Spring 2009 edition of Sonoma Magazine I was surprised to see that one of the featured homes in the Pacific Union ad was one that we had lived in for a year and a half. The reason that we lived there is in other stories. Enough to say now is that in July 1996 we had decided to live in California so had sold our Pittsburgh house, and our furniture was in storage. Dad Coops' house had been sold to settle the estate and we were in the process of buying an acre of the property to build a house.

Real Estate ad for Fred's House

I had written to Fred Nilson, one of Dad Coops' "Lunch Bunch" buddies. We had become acquainted because we always took Dad Coops for his weekly lunches with his friends. Fred had a big house on Loma Vista, off Arnold Drive, near Sonoma. This 140-year-old house had a 100-year-old addition, which was a complete apartment. I asked him if we could live there for a while. He was a little reluctant because his son sometimes came on weekends and used it. We made an agreement that we would go somewhere else anytime John needed it. He agreed, we moved in, and it was the beginning of an extraordinary one-and-a-half years.

One day I was sitting on the huge wraparound porch and looking out onto the "most beautiful four acres in Sonoma County," as Fred described it. There were at least a dozen Valley Oaks within sight and it was a lovely setting, but I was feeling rather bleak. For four years we had been living in Dad Coops' spacious house, and taking respite breaks back in our Pittsburgh home where we had our own things and our other car. Now I didn't know how long it would take to have our new house built.

But soon we started to very much enjoy both Fred and his house. He told stories about his life from the time he was a poor orphan boy in Philadelphia, and how he had left to seek his fortune. A born salesman, he did indeed become very wealthy in California as he became successful in the real estate and wholesale liquor businesses.

He was now 90 years old, but still able to live alone. He had two Cadillacs, which he often drove. Sometimes the Sonoma Airporter would come and take him to SFO for a visit to a Five Star hotel in Hawaii or to visit his daughter and granddaughters in southern California.

Fred was away the night we watched a magnificent sky show. Not only was the Hale-Bopp comet in the sky, but also an eclipse of the moon, and at the same time the planet Mars was especially close and bright. We took binoculars, lawn chairs, and hot chocolate out into the dark field near the house and watched the displays. It was an exceptional treat to see Hale-Bopp because the comet isn't scheduled to return for another 2380 years, and it was only 1997.

Fred had owned the Loma Vista property for many years and the farm house was the family's summer home. Fred had developed that area, and called himself the "Squire of Loma Vista." His real estate specialty was buying "raw land," which could be developed. About 10 years before, he and his wife had decided to sell their San Francisco home and move to Sonoma and fix up the old farm house. Unfortunately, she died only a month after the move so few improvements had been made.

It seemed to us that he was inordinately proud of the shabby old house, but it filled his needs perfectly and he loved it. When I went over to his side of the house, I went through a door in our bedroom to the large "library." Next was the unused cobweb-decked dining room and near it was a clothes closet with fine, but moth-eaten, garments. I went past two rarely used bedrooms, the living room, and then into the antique kitchen where he fixed his healthy breakfasts. "Five fruits every morning and an egg or some cereal, and have a highball with your dinner" was his advice. He had arranged to have his dinners prepared by a Sonoma caterer. As time went by I frequently took food to him. Art took care of chores around the house. Once when both we and Fred planned to be away for a couple of days Art set off some bug bombs in the moth-infested areas of the house. Fred was quite appreciative of that project and thanked us profusely.

He often invited us to his large room upstairs. To arrive there it was necessary to proceed up a narrow and rather precarious stairway. The room had a lovely view across the valley and over to the mountains. Sometime in the past Fred had arranged for two bedrooms to be combined into one large room as a surprise for his wife. This was the only improved part of the house. It was a pleasant room where he enjoyed TV, reading, and writing. His bedroom and bath were across the hall.

Our kitchen and bath were unique. I cooked on a vintage but efficient Wedgewood propane gas-powered stove, which even had an accurate oven. One section of the stove was built to burn wood or coal, but an inspection of the chimney showed that it would be unwise to start a fire. Off the kitchen there was a small ramshackle closed-in back porch with laundry tubs, but no laundry. I took clothes to the laundromat. The bathroom was directly off the kitchen and was equipped with a claw foot tub, and also a separate shower that John had installed. The only heat in the apartment was a small electric heater in the bathroom and a propane gas heater in the living room. We used fans for summer cooling.

We took Fred for his eye doctor appointments in San Francisco. We benefitted, too, because he always took us for a lovely lunch and then perhaps a museum or other point of interest. After seeing the Rodin ex-hibit I decided that sculpture was one of my favorite art forms. Another trip that he thoroughly enjoyed was going to Clear Lake where he had started his California real estate career by selling lots at a summer resort. Revisiting this area led to his being asked to write a series of stories for the Clear Lake paper, an assignment that he was thrilled to do. He enjoyed telling about being the center of attention as the "eastern dude."

Each spring there was the ritual of getting out his enormous blue 1973 Cadillac convertible and putting the top down for the summer. Sometimes he would take us for a ride and, once in a while, step on the gas to show us how fast it would go. That was a mixed pleasure. A couple of times Art drove the car in a Sonoma parade, and the distinguished passengers waved to the spectators. For trips such as to San Francisco or Clear Lake, Art drove "Big Red," the 1986 Coupe de Ville.

We had told Fred that we would need to stay at his house for only a short time. But as the months went by he teased us about being the "folks who came to dinner." He didn't mind that we were there because he

Fred, his house, and car

needed help now as well as enjoying having somebody to talk to because many of his contemporaries were no longer living. His son never asked us to relinquish his space. He often told us how much he disliked the house, and it seemed to be a relief to him to stay in his RV when he came to visit. Fred's daughter never came, but they talked regularly on the phone.

Our mailing address was still a P.O. box in Kenwood so we were there almost every day. The big old storage barn had Dad Coops' office in one corner, so sometimes I went there to do paperwork. It seemed like one place that was sort of our own.

Knowing Fred and living at 84 Loma Vista gave us a glimpse into a different world. The new 84 Loma Vista house has little of the original construction or room arrangement, but still has the same size and shape. We could live there again for $3,950,000.

◄◄ | ►►

1996-1997 "HOW MUCH LONGER?"

Art's brother, Melvin, was on firm legal ground in claiming an equal right to buy an acre from their father's estate. Melvin had instructed his lawyer that no matter what we bid, he was to bid $1000 more. We couldn't afford to play his bidding game.

Art talked to Kathy and Ray Yahr to see if they could consider buying the entire property from the estate and then selling an acre to us. Since they were planning to sell it anyway they agreed. We went back to Plan A, which triggered many complications.

Melvin filed a 9-page, 18-point objection to letting us buy the land. Our lawyer wrote a great rebuttal and enclosed Art and Melvin's sister Betty's letter of support for us. A negotiation meeting and hearing were scheduled for the next week but were cancelled.

It isn't clear in my mind the exact order of good and bad events. It was two steps forward and one back in getting things settled. For Thanksgiving we drove to Soquel, near Santa Cruz, to celebrate with Art's cousin and family. Kathy and Ray invited us to have Christmas dinner with them. We were back in Dad Coops' old house with a new cast of characters.

With all our wonderful friends and family it was so sad that problems with Melvin dominated our time and energy. We still had to pay the estate 1½ years of rent because we had lived in Dad Coops' house after he died and repairs had been completed. The law was on Melvin's side in this matter, too. Our two years of caretaking that had allowed Dad Coops to live in his own home and had saved the estate a lot of money couldn't legally be counted in negotiations.

Our lawyer had a solution. He explained that the executor of an estate has wide latitude for being reimbursed for expenses. Art should submit a list of "extraordinary" expenses. We spent hours writing down everything connected with taking care of the property, repairing it, and putting it on the market. We managed to get up to the number that Melvin said we should pay for rent.

The agreement was submitted for Melvin's approval but his lawyer said he was on vacation. Evidently his vacation was spent writing a 25-page objection and he wanted thousands of dollars. My hopes were fading along with any hope of having a house built.

However, we found that all Melvin really wanted was the list of expenses withdrawn. That cancelled out the rent demands, which had been the purpose of the whole exercise. At one point I asked our lawyer, "How much longer can Melvin torture us?" He replied matter-of-factly, "Oh, it will be a while yet." For him it was all in a day's work. Melvin still wanted a trial. It was never clear to me what the charges would be.

It was appropriate that the final settlement hearing was on April Fools' Day. We went through the security line at the court house and took our places. A bored judge listened and said there wasn't much to it, and to go to the conference room and work it out. At one point I was sitting all alone in the big courtroom while folks negotiated. Art and our lawyer came back and we just chatted for a while. I was thinking it was a very expensive chat.

The court investigator came and said that Melvin was in a highly emotional state and wouldn't talk anymore. He still wanted a trial about his grievances, whatever they were. If that happened there wouldn't be any estate left. Finally it was determined that Melvin could be bought off for $5000, which seemed like a bargain. Art agreed. Melvin was mollified, but then upset that he had to give half of it to their sister.

Finally, there was a settlement. I felt an enormous peace come over me. But Melvin was still living rent-free in my head and I needed to evict the unwelcome tenant. That should have been easy because we had many other things to think about.

Since Kathy and Ray had to buy the house and three acres, it was necessary to renegotiate their mortgage. Kathy's mother said she wouldn't live in the cottage in its present condition. "Repairs" turned out to be a complete rebuilding of the cottage. All that was left of the original was part of the water tower. Dry rot had been extensive.

At the same time we were having our problems with the County. They required a test that showed 48" of topsoil, which was good, but the volcanic soil drained much too fast. They said to spread fill dirt over the large septic area to make it all a foot higher. The ground water was unusually high that year. We had optimistically obtained a building permit but weren't yet able to use it.

1997-1998 MIRACLE HOUSE

We had finally made our way through the numerous roadblocks to building a house. The first hurdle had been to clear our purchase of an acre of estate property. If the other people who were interested in the house and three acres had bought it, instead of Ray and Kathy Yahr, they wouldn't have sold any of it.

Hoped-for building site on Greene Street in Kenwood

"Splitting off an acre" in county-speak turned out to be "creating a minor sub-division" with all the accompanying regulations. The extra-wet spring of 1997 made it difficult to pass the drainage requirements. One test was to get somebody with a backhoe to dig and reveal the soil profile. Apparently this showed that our soil would drain so fast that contamination would get into the ground water. The rule said we had to put twelve more inches of fill dirt over the drain field. The man who laid our leach line said we probably needed only about a third of the required length.

Finally the County was satisfied but Art's brother definitely wasn't. We endured a steady stream of threats and legal maneuvers. Finally everything was settled but by then our building permit had expired. The County said we had to re-apply and start all over. It was time to talk to

143

somebody with authority. We made an appointment with Mike Cale, a County Supervisor. He was sympathetic and said he would support an extension of our building permit. When one of the County people said we had to do something or other, it was so satisfying to say, "No, Mike said this would be okay."

We'd had plenty of time to peruse dozens of floor plans. I wanted a sunroom on a second floor such as the one I had enjoyed so much in Dad Coops' house. But financial reality eliminated a two-story house. It probably wouldn't have been a good idea anyway. I needed to choose a plan very carefully, because with Art when something is done, it's done.

House orientation was important in the matchless Sonoma Valley location. We stood on the lot and looked in every direction to decide where and how we could best take advantage of the views. Dad Coops' 80' long equipment storage shed in back was another consideration.

Our builder, Jim Dawson, had an artistic bent. He enjoyed designing on the computer. Art was making drawings, too, and a house quite similar to the two we'd had in Pennsylvania was developing. Jim suggested that the porch go around both front corners of the house instead of just one, to "balance it."

The first sign of a real house appeared when a white outline was drawn on the ground showing its size and shape. That was very exciting! In September 1997, ground was finally broken. The concrete for our footer was to be delivered on a Monday. On Sunday the last hymn at church was "How Firm a Foundation." Fred Nilson, whose house we were still living in, said the hymn should have been dedicated to us.

Sub flooring came next. One day Art and I were checking the dimensions, and the numbers weren't adding up. We told Jim and he found that he had made the foundation 8" longer than the plan. If it had been 8" shorter we would have been upset, but this mistake was good, although not confidence-inspiring.

It was a wet winter. Art often swept water off the sub floor. But the whole compound was making good progress. The rebuilt cottage was cozy and comfortable, and Kathy and Ray Yahr were making the necessary changes for opening a bed and breakfast. Three of the bedroom walk-in closets were made into bathrooms. The fourth bedroom and the sun porch were now a suite that used the original bathroom. Kathy and

Ray worked hard hanging new wallpaper and painting.

The Yahrs and Kathy's parents, the Mitchells, all became our good friends. I saw Frank and Marcia Mitchell almost every day as we shared newspapers. Frank and Art both enjoyed being outdoors.

We traveled to Arizona to spend Thanksgiving with Art's sister and family, and the next month went to Soquel for Christmas with Art's cousin's family. There was reason to be optimistic about the new year, 1998. We would finally have a California house of our own. Another coming event was that son Dan and Amy were expecting their first baby in September. That would be our seventh grandchild.

The constant rain was a detriment to building. Some people were suffering severe flooding. But good progress had been made on our house. In February we had new tax bills and County approval to move in. On March first our furniture finally came out of storage, and there were piles of boxes everywhere.

Fred had teased us about staying at his house so long but now he didn't want us to leave. He had reached an age when he shouldn't live alone. A young couple was moving into his apartment. They, along with Bill Morris and his friend, helped us move from Fred's to our new Kenwood house.

It was a light, bright house, a little over 1500 sq. ft. I had decided to have white kitchen cabinets, which Jim built for us. Two cabinets had glass fronts. The kitchen turned out to be larger than I had expected. There was room for a pantry cupboard and a small desk. Except for the kitchen and bathrooms, the floors were carpeted in a warm, delicious nutmeg color. Jim built the cabinets for the bathrooms, too. The bathrooms weren't large, but oversize mirrors gave the illusion of more space.

We made endless trips to Santa Rosa stores to choose appliances, floor and window coverings, countertops, lights, windows, ceiling fan, paint colors, roof shingles, etc. I never wanted to go to Home Depot again. Our choices were mostly satisfactory. Our house was "Pacific Blue" and had a "Stormy Weather" roof, grey with a little blue. Interior walls were basic off-white.

We had seen a house with the third bedroom accessible through an archway on one wall, as well as having a regular door to the hall. This idea worked well for us. My sewing machine was placed there, and also a sofa bed. A "great room" accommodated the dining room table and china cupboard as well as the living room furniture, TV, and a gas log stove in the corner. Two other bedrooms and two baths completed the house design. The detached garage was located behind the house. Regulations required a larger garage than we had planned because of the earthquake rules.

The plan didn't allow many choices for where to arrange furniture. Two bedroom windows were spaced so the king-sized bed would fit between them. There was only one usable place in the dining area for the corner shelves. I'm not a furniture re-arranger so it would have been almost safe to nail things down.

I had a place for my mother's old and artistically designed White sewing machine, a popular brand in its time. Above it was a good space to hang a large ornately-framed portrait of my fraternal grandmother and her three sisters. Other inherited pieces included a refinished chest and bookshelves from the Shannon family farm. The work table from the farm "pump house" went on the porch. We could eat out there in nice weather.

The kitchen eating area table and chairs were in Dad Coops' house. Before that they were in his parents' home. I had always liked Cathryn's dry sink that she had in the laundry room. It held her detergent and other supplies. We were able to get it for our house and place it in a more prominent position. We also received a coat rack that we put near the front door. A coat closet is there, too. Dad Coops' old marble-top dresser fit into the guest room. Art thought the dresser was ugly but I liked it.

We hung my first quilt on a wall in the guest room. Many family photographs are on the hallway walls. Other wall hangings include a reproduction of a painting similar to Art's Danish great-grandfather sea captain's sailing ship. We had a collection of colorful fruit box labels which are displayed on the wall by the dining table. Several of the labels were designed by Art's grandfather and bear the inscription "Coops Bros.," Art's father and uncle.

I used many of my quilted wall hangings around the house. I liked clocks, and I made one with a counted cross-stitch face. My wall-sized Mickey Mouse watch hangs in the sewing room. We also have several of our daughters' paintings.

The wrap-around front porch is long but not deep so doesn't accommodate thirty people as the one on Dad's house did. But it's very comfortable for a few folks. The back deck isn't large either, but the grape

146

arbor over it provides another shady spot.

Art was soon busy planting shade trees, fruit trees, and a vegetable garden. He gradually added shrubs and flowers around the house. He was outside most of the time with his digging, planting, weeding, pruning, etc. We bought an old farm tractor and he broke up the ground with the disc. I said he was working too hard and he said, "I'm out in the sunshine and I'm having fun."

We started to have company right away as soon as we moved in, and it continued all year. First I had a party for Fred, Yahrs, and Mitchells. The next month, daughter Alison and her three little children visited from Frederick, Maryland. Lauren, the youngest, was not quite two. Jessica and Andrew were about eight and five. It seemed that every month somebody else came to visit.

We traveled, too, going to Mercer, Pennsylvania, and my 50th high school reunion. It felt as though our house was really "home" when we returned from our trip. I said, "I didn't remember how pretty it is!"

Kenwood house - finally
Praise the Lord! I prayed a lot!

Somebody asked if we had remodeled an old house. It looked as though it had always been there, our blue house on Greene Street.

Red-haired baby grandson, Ryan, added to Vermont color in September. It was a perfect time to take a trip to Burlington. He was another adorable grandchild and we felt very fortunate. In November daughter Dinah, Steve, and little Tess came to Kenwood for Thanksgiving. The next month we had our first Christmas in our own California

147

house. I asked Art if there was anything else special about our house. He said, "It's paid for."

The next couple of years brought growth of all kinds. Kathy and Ray were ready for their first guests at the bed and breakfast, which they decided to name Muir Manor after an ancestor of Kathy's, John Muir.

Brendan, another son for Dan and Amy, arrived on June 10, 2000, the only grandchild born in the 21st century. He was our eighth and last. We watched as the children grew and thrived.

I want to dedicate our "Miracle House" to:
Art's father, Arthur August Coops and his wife,
Cathryn Cleland Coops
Art's sister, Betty Coops James
Kathy and Ray Yahr
Bill Morris
Fred Nilson
Sonoma attorney, Charles Harris
Santa Rosa attorney David Bjornstrom
of Anderson, Zeigler, Disharoon, Gallagher, & Gray law firm
Court Investigator who helped obtain Art's Conservatorship,
and later the final agreement
Shearson Smith Barney investment advisor in Pittsburgh who helped
freeze accounts until estate matters were settled.
Mike Cale, County Supervisor

PART SIX:
THE TURN OF THE CENTURY

DIVORCE DID THEM PART

Art's sister, Betty Coops James, lived in Sierra Vista, Arizona, which is near Tucson. She lived near her daughter, Cindy James Subia, and Cindy's husband, Dan, and their four children. It was good to see this part of the family and was also nice to be in Arizona in February. This visit was in 2000.

Betty Coops James

Betty's husband, Ed, had died recently and, sad to say, she appeared to be happier. She said she had girlfriends for the first time in many years. Ed was jealous and controlling with her. But he had always been pleasant and hospitable to us and we had no reason to dislike him. He adored his daughter, Cindy, and her older son, Edward.

The families attended the Church of the Nazarene. It was a large church with three services and Sunday School classes. Betty's adult education class was unlike any I had ever attended. It seemed to be part revival meeting and part therapy session. A person who had a particular need sat in the middle and other class members laid on hands and prayed for the petitioner. We heard a variety of sad stories and it looked as though the sufferers were helped. I felt like saying I was thankful our family was doing well.

I'm glad I didn't say anything because when we got home there was a very disturbing e-mail from Melinda. She said she had filed for a "protection from abuse" and Michael was ordered out of the house. I was stunned but she seemed relieved and almost ecstatic that he was gone.

Both Betty and Melinda were kind souls who had married control freaks, but Betty and Melinda were entirely different types of people. Betty stayed married but told me later that she thought Melinda had done the right thing. Melinda had self-esteem while Betty did not, even though Betty, too, was a bright, talented person who was capable of supporting herself.

I hadn't realized that Melinda was so unhappy. She and Michael

151

had been married for 20 years and had two wonderful boys. I had been concerned when Michael spoke so sharply to her and I thought I've known Melinda for a long time and she isn't one to put up with that. But I never expected divorce. She said the first ten years had been good but she could see that the marriage was in trouble. While she was "just a wife," taking care of the children, enjoying her oil painting, and doing volunteer work everything was fine. But as she moved into the business world and found success Michael was jealous and believed he was losing control. He could see that Melinda could live without him and was afraid she would leave. With this fear he became violent and tried to force her to stay. His behavior scared Melinda to the point where she knew it was necessary to get away from him.

Michael's ego was shattered. He was a very intelligent man, a devout Roman Catholic, and a college professor who was respected in his field. A divorce didn't fit his profile. He hired a lawyer and was determined to fight the divorce action.

Many difficult months of court appearances followed. Melinda couldn't have done it without the help of her lawyer-friend, Susan. At first Melinda had feared for her safety but gradually agreements were reached. These resulted in some unusual circumstances. Michael was living across the street with a mutual friend of both of them. The boys were sometimes in one house and sometimes in the other.

Michael wanted the house, so he bought Melinda's share. This allowed her to buy a house of her own. Now the boys stayed in their own rooms again and the parents moved back and forth between the two houses. This continued until Patrick was sixteen and could drive. Then Melinda moved out completely.

It had been a good house and location for raising a family. Both the elementary and high schools were within easy walking distance. Only middle school required a bus ride. The parents both took great pride in their sons and their activities. I thought Melinda was a wonderful mother. She understood boys and guided them adroitly without using a heavy hand.

Jonathan sailed through his academic work and Patrick was a star on the athletic field. It was a pleasure to watch them grow and progress. After visiting a number of colleges they both decided to go to the University of Pittsburgh, where their father taught. This was also a financial advantage.

Melinda was making progress in her career. She worked with an international organization, Supply Chain, eventually helping to arrange conferences all over the world. Some of the places her work took her were South Africa, Australia, Singapore, Belgium, and Prague. She often worked in Washington, D.C. and eventually bought a condo in Annandale, but lived and worked in Pittsburgh, too.

I don't have either a happy ending or sad ending. This is a story in progress.

◄◄ | ►►

FIRST-CLASS OBSESSION

It had been a good week, June 9-16, 2009, in Richmond, Virginia. We visited our daughter, Alison, her husband Chuck Ludwig, and our three grandchildren, Jessica, Andrew, and Lauren. The special event was oldest granddaughter Jessica's high school graduation and the activities connected with it. Her school was called Deep Run, the grammar school was Short Pump, another district Three Chopt, and Pocahontas was nearby.

Jessica Ludwig
H.S. Graduation 2009

Teenagers were everywhere, 433 graduating seniors and then Jessica's high school and church friends coming to her party a couple of days later. I helped Alison bake cookies and make other desserts for the party. Then she made salads, dips, and other picnic style food for the barbeque supper.

We were accustomed to seeing our friends with various shapes of hearing aids in their ears and these young people also often wore earpieces but theirs were for their iPods. It was common to see the young folks carrying cell phones for their nonstop texting. Phones vibrated instead of ringing. We sometimes had trouble communicating with young people because they talked so fast and softly while we're slower and hearing impaired. But we enjoyed the youngsters, who seemed like delightful and puzzling combinations of children and wise adults, all in the same bodies. These young bodies were overflowing with boundless energy.

Our oldest daughter, Melinda, drove from Pittsburgh to spend a couple of days with us, and it was wonderful to see her again. It was fun to have a car full of people going to church. Once we even had to take two cars when we all went out to eat.

Soon it was time to go back to our own world and Chuck took us to the airport. I had made the plane reservations several months before and had used bonus miles to upgrade to first class. Our trip to Richmond had been in this unaccustomed luxury and I was looking forward to more of the same going back.

First there's always the security torture and this time I met a new machine. My number came up to step into this thing that looked like a "cone of silence." There were two sets of footprints, one set one way and another set the other direction. "Arms up, turn, arms front" as a scanner swung around. The guard said, "Do you have something in your right pocket?" I said it was tip money and pulled out the money clip. The guard spoke into his microphone. "It's a clip with cash... I said cash." I was released to retrieve my shoes and bags. Art only had to drop his suspenders this time. Once he had to take off both his suspenders and belt, so he had to walk carefully through the scanner.

We had plenty of time for a leisurely lunch, too much time. Our plane to Philadelphia was late. The man at the gate announced that it wouldn't take long to unload and reload and our connecting flights wouldn't be in jeopardy. We finally got aboard and found our seats.

It was only an hour flight. As we approached Philadelphia we asked the flight attendant about our departure gate, which on the airport map looked far from where we would land. She said to turn left when we got off the plane, go to F10 and get on the shuttle bus to A, B, and C concourses. The man behind us said he had done it lots of times and would help us. We had to stand on the crowded bus, and then walk and walk. We found that the nice young man was a NASCAR photographer and was headed to Sonoma Raceway at Sears Point. He stuck with us all the way to our gate, which we found quiet and empty. The plane had left nine minutes early and somebody else got our first class seats!

The NASCAR man said that he thought he saw our plane pulling away while we were on the bus. I felt devastated. We went to Customer Service and got put on the next flight to SFO, which was about two hours later with no first class available. I was very close to tears. The nice NASCAR man decided to wait for the flight after that and get his first class seat, but that was getting very late. Besides, there weren't two more seats in first class.

We told our troubles to the attendant at our new gate and he was sympathetic, but his only suggestion was to try to kidnap a couple of folks who had first class seats and get them out of the way. We sat down and the lady beside me heard me wailing into my phone. She had many encouraging words and said my glass was still half full. She spoke very positively.

The gatekeeper had another joke as we showed our boarding passes, but I couldn't hear what he said. He was a cheerful fellow. As we got on the plane, I mentioned to the flight attendant that we had lost our first class seats. She was sympathetic,too, and said she would keep it in mind. Our seats were in row 8. After I got settled I decided that wasn't too bad and we would get home just as well. A man came to take the aisle seat and of course I told him about my disappointment. He was sorry about that, and also sorry that he wasn't able to sit with his wife. I said people are usually nice about switching, and that's what happened. Now his wife knew about my distress, too.

A few minutes before takeoff the jovial door attendant came and asked, "Are you the folks who had first class tickets?" We said we certainly were. Enough people knew about it now that there were smiles all around. We gathered up our belongings and went forward where I joyfully dropped into a first class seat. We took off on time and I appreciated the extra amenities all the way across the country.

We had a beautifully soft on-time landing, were happy to find our baggage had come with us, called the motel shuttle, got our car, and were on our way home. I had been prepared to write a letter to US Airways enumerating our troubles, but now I should write something complimentary about their personnel and accommodations.

We were thankful for the long hours of light in June. The Golden Gate Bridge is always impressive but at dusk with lights coming on in the city the sight was magical. The traffic wasn't bad and there was still a touch of light in the sky when we arrived in Kenwood.

I walked into our house with a sense of wonderment and relief. It was a happy ending to a very long day.

HAROLD VAN COOPS 1919-2009

Stories that Art told from their Sonoma childhoods sometimes involved his oldest cousin Harold's difficulties with keeping out of trouble. Occasional fires and explosions resulted from Harold's insatiable curiosity about the fascinating works of nature. Even his name was different than the rest of the family. He decided to take his father's middle name, Van, and make it part of his last name.

His parents recognized that they had a son with some exceptional abilities and started schooling him at an early age. He had already mastered a number of subjects by the time he started public school. Evidently this presented a problem for the school and for Harold. He skipped three grades as he went along and this made social adjustment difficult even though the academic work was no problem.

By age sixteen, he had graduated with honors from high school and was accepted by the University of California at Berkeley. He was dili-gent in his studies. At the same time a young co-ed captured his heart. He told about wearing his pencil down to a nubbin because he kept going to sharpen his pencil so he could walk by Marguerite.

To his father's consternation the romance blossomed. He couldn't picture himself with a Mexican Catholic daughter-in-law. Marguerite's family wasn't happy either. Both fami-lies had high expectations for their children. Marguerite's father wanted her to be a doctor. Objections were

Harry and Marguerite Van Coops 1975

so vehement that Harry and Marguerite were married secretly. He was 21 and she was 20. Harry's father eventually admitted that Marguerite was the best thing that ever happened to his son. Harold was a gentle and caring soul and Marguerite brought out the best in him.

The marriage was in 1940. Education funds were cut off so Harry got a job at the Mare Island Naval shipyard. He survived a serious accident there. After his recovery he enlisted in the army. That was in 1943, the same year that Marguerite gave birth to a son. WWII interrupted their lives and Harry served four years in Italy in the Medical Corps. When he came back he completed his education and graduated with a B.S. degree from the Cal Berkeley School of Public Health.

By the time I met Harry and Marguerite they were the parents of several children. On visits to California we occasionally saw them at Harry's parents' home, Cheery Acres, in Sonoma. Sometimes we saw them when they came to Kenwood. He seemed to me to be a great dad as he played ball with his boys and attended to their needs. Through the years we, with our growing family, saw them with their growing family. We were able to go to their only daughter's wedding and coincidentally they came to our only son's wedding. Marguerite and Harry had four sons and one daughter and we had three daughters and one son.

Marguerite and I shared an interest in quilting. She was a professional, and qualified to teach quilting. I marveled at her skill. I remember attending a quilt show with her and then going to a fabric shop. The four of us had many good times.

Harry retired from the Alameda County Health Department in 1982 and they moved to Lompoc, which they found to be a great retirement spot. Harry had embraced the Roman Catholic faith and they were active members of the Queen of Angels Church where he sang in the choir.

They were founding members of the La Purisima Mission's Visitor Center and served as docents for many years. Harry restored the herb garden in the self-sustaining mission and he was taking care of it when we visited there. Marguerite made Spanish language tapes for visitors. She spoke beautiful melodious Spanish.

Harry was in failing health for the last few years and Marguerite tenderly cared for him. He died on July 24, 2009. Their 69th wedding anniversary would have been in December.

We decided to go to the funeral although I was concerned about the nearly 350 mile drive to Lompoc, which is almost to Santa Barbara. We drove there on July 31 and stayed at a motel with a large contingent of other Coops relatives. It was a sad occasion but we had a marvelous reunion. Two of Harry's three siblings were there and many of his ten grandchildren and five great-grandchildren. Eight of us had reservations to eat at a Lompoc restaurant. We noticed another table set for eight beside us. When they came in we were all surprised to see it was yet another branch of Harry and Marguerite's family. There were hugs and hellos all around. I especially enjoyed becoming better acquainted with people that I had seen only briefly at other family events.

Harry Van Coops

The Mass of Christian Burial was celebrated the morning of August 1. The cemetery was at Arroyo Grande, about 40 miles to the north. We rode with a cousin who was following another cousin who was following Mapquest. We were puzzled to find ourselves on a twisting mountain road. We had gone past Arroyo Grande on the way to Lompoc, and the highway had been perfectly fine. Mapquest isn't infallible. We had an easier trip back to the church for the reception. After another sociable dinner that evening we drove home the next day, happy that we had participated.

CHURCH BAZAARS

It started small. A group of us among the younger women in the Sharon, Pennsylvania, Presbyterian Church decided to form a study, service, and worship group. We meant "younger." We thought women over 35 would probably be too old. We decided to name the group "Wishart Circle" in honor of the pastor's wonderful wife. They had been at that church for years and were highly respected in the community.

As with most groups who want to do "good works," fund raising became a large part of the activity. Why not make and sell a few crafts at church suppers, which would be a slightly larger project than the traditional bake sale?

As the years went by and even we were over 35, we had decided it would be good to include everybody. Our little project had grown and grown. It now needed the gymnasium, dining room, stage, kitchen, and a couple of other rooms to provide enough space for the numerous booths. It became so popular that people waited outside for the doors to open. Each bazaar had a theme with appropriate decorations to match. We often wore special outfits, too, such as fancy hats or long skirts.

Booths included aprons, a bake shop, books, children's items, handcrafts devoted to the Christmas theme: candy, cheese, cookbooks, country kitchen, trash and treasure, and gifts. The men had their own workshop creations. The kitchen and dining room were bustling as they served both lunch and dinner.

All this activity required many committees: decorating and posters, table decorations, coffee bar, door greeters, telephone, newspapers, radio, childcare, name tags (yes, we even had theme-decorated tags), and Wednesday workshops. One year I was co-chairman and I'll never fully recover. The other woman in charge was creative and had an idea-a-minute mind. I think she could have been C.E.O. of a corporation. We cleared over $10,000, which was very good in 1974.

One of our more unusual projects was to go to the cemetery dump and rescue the beautiful wreaths that had been tossed there. A friend said,

"Here comes Marge. She has everything in her station wagon except the Amishman's horse!" One year I made many Christmas wreaths. Another year I sewed numerous aprons because they were good sellers then. Pillows were popular, too, and I liked making them.

Shirley and wreaths 1980

When we had a meeting to discuss how to put the money to good use, it seemed to be almost as hard to spend wisely as it was to earn the money. We gave portions locally, nationally, and internationally. Among community recipients might be Meals-on-Wheels and the Domestic Violence Center. National organizations could include Theological Seminaries, the West Virginia Mountain Project, or the National Parks Ministry. International needs once included Latin American Mission Projects and the Korean Scholarship Fund. Church World Service was often a recipient.

The bazaars were still going on when we moved to Pittsburgh. The church there didn't do bazaars so I had about nine years off before we came to California. For several years we were busy looking after Dad Coops and then getting settled into our own home. I was aware that the Sonoma United Methodist Church, which we had been attending, had bazaars, too, and I started to help with a few things. Younger women

161

don't have the time or interest to devote so many hours to the same kind of projects that had been done in the past.

Although there were still many hand-crafted items such as quilts, embroidery, and knit goods made by church members, at the more recent bazaars alternative gifts were included. Opportunities were presented for choosing gifts that carried the promise of providing tools, blankets, and animals for people everywhere who were in need. This was done through Church World Service.

One church couple, Sandra and Gordon Metzger, had traveled extensively on their Volunteers in Mission trips. Super-shopper Sandra chose a variety of items, many of which were made by women and children. These often very small businesses helped to maintain the families. Gordon and Sandra's "store" grew dramatically to include warm jackets, hats, sweaters, and vests. Exquisite and unique jewelry and carved animals covered several tables. The Bazaar provided one of the venues for displaying and selling goods for which the artists received fair prices. "Fair Trade" coffee, tea, and chocolate also guaranteed that farmers got a fair share of the return for their produce.

The Heifer Project is at least 65 years old. Young milk cows have been distributed all over the world. When a milking cow is given to a poverty-stricken family, it can produce as much as four gallons of milk a day, plenty to drink and some to sell. That family then passes on a female calf to another family. A Heifer Project gift can benefit many generations. Under the sponsorship of Heifer Project, there were other choices such as sending bees, sheep, goats, alpacas, llamas, chicks, pigs, rabbits, ducks, or geese.

Evolution and revolution have changed the bazaar agenda. But there is still a feeling of accomplishment and satisfaction when one sees a room aglow and bursting with beautiful items, decorated dining tables, and bustling activity. However, after nearly 40 years of bazaar work, I have an "enough is enough" feeling.

THE FOLKS WHERE WE LIVE

Retirement usually brings changes to people's lives, but ours seemed to be drastic. We had expected to be in California for perhaps six months while we looked after Dad Coops in his last days. However, he lived for two more years and we became ever more settled in Kenwood.

The village of Kenwood is on Route 12, halfway between Sonoma and Santa Rosa. It was quite different than anywhere we had lived before. The mountain scenery was spectacular, and there were many nationally and internationally known wineries in the valley between the two mountain ranges. But those aren't the differences that I mean. Eastern neighborhoods were more consistent in having similar houses with similar styles of upkeep grouped together. On streets in Kenwood we noticed well-kept houses next to ones that looked neglected. Perhaps upkeep was more difficult in the dry summers, or maybe it was just California with its casual lifestyle.

County government appeared to be inconsistent, too. While rules were strict about new construction, a decrepit old building was allowed to stand. The eyesore was a burnt out yellowish house, which sat prominently as one approached Kenwood from Sonoma.

We walked around the village almost daily and became acquainted and reacquainted with people in the area. We had heard about an October event called ARTrails and wanted to know where the two Kenwood artists lived. One artist, basket-maker Susan Miron, lived on the next street and her backyard nearly adjoined ours. A fence made it necessary to walk about three blocks to get to the front of her house. We had noticed the small, separate building, which often had lights on late at night. We found that it was her workshop where she made her intricate baskets. Her husband, Dr. Nathan Miron, an amateur astronomer, wrote a column, Star Spangled Banter, for the Kenwood Press.

Judy and Ray Watten were the other Kenwood artists. They lived on Maple Avenue, which was about six blocks from our house. When we reached the Watten home a woman was working in the front yard. I asked,

"Are you the artist?" She assured us, "We try to be." Judy remembers it a bit differently. She said that she and Ray noticed people looking at her garden and came out to talk. However it happened it was a fortuitous meeting.

In the days after the ARTrails exhibit we saw Judy and Ray Watten from time to time as we went on our walks. Once they had an exhibit of Japanese garments and I bought a haori (HA-o-ri), a jacket that is made kimono-style. It's lapped left to right in front rather than our customary right to left. I got compliments every time I wore it.

One day they invited us into their house and we found a small museum of artifacts from different parts of the world. Gradually we heard bits and pieces of their worldwide adventures. It was years before I heard the full story of Judy's front yard, a "Japanified" Zen garden. Water is the theme of these gardens, whether there's water or not. Judy had a dry creek. It took years of hard work to get the garden to conform to her plan. Ray liked to work in his backyard garden where he started plants early in a cold frame, and the crops continued to the end of the season.

Judy was one of the instigators who convinced me that going to Curves would be good for me. She also said that I would like the Life Story Writing Class that meets weekly in Oakmont. Since it was a project I had been considering I started to attend in September 2008. That's when I really got Judy's inside stories, the kind that wouldn't come out in casual conversation.

Other neighbors include Ellen who lived across the street. She often invited us to come and swim in her pool. She would say in her thick German accent, "Shir-LEE, why don't you like water? You came once and hardly got in." She enjoyed showing the outdoor amenities around her pool, and her house with its many ornate knick-knacks.

Barb lived across from Ellen. The first time I talked to her she was in great distress because her sister had just died from a heart attack. Barb suffered many sorrows, including losing one of her two sons, and her husband dying from ALS. She found an emotional outlet in dancing. She lost a lot of weight and now cuts quite a figure on the dance floor.

Liz Parsons wrote a gardening column in the Kenwood Press. One day when we were walking on a neighborhood road, Turtle Creek, she invited us to come through the gate and see their property. Liz was a native plant enthusiast and there were many wild flowers in her collections. Some of the flowers grew along the bank leading down to the Sonoma Creek. I don't know why their street was called Turtle Creek. Partner Milt was a mulch enthusiast. He showed us how he could dig potatoes with his hands because the ground was so soft.

Genevie lived down the street. Through the years she had worked for Dad Coops and helped with housework. She was a marvelous gardener and cook. She preserved much of her garden and orchard produce for winter use. We often stopped in to visit and missed her when she sold her house and moved to a retirement community in Santa Rosa.

There were other neighbors that we knew casually because we became somewhat acquainted when we were out walking.

The year 2004 brought many changes to the neighborhood. I was distressed when Kathy and Ray Yahr decided to put the bed and breakfast on the market. We always got along so well with them and were anxious about any changes. For instance, the water supply from Dad Coops' well had piping that extended into what was now our property. Art had been using it for watering his garden. But they received $2,000,000 for the bed and breakfast, which should cover their high expenses for the conversion of the house.

The day came when the moving van arrived. I went over to the cottage and saw Frank and Marcia sitting among piles of boxes. It was very sad and I couldn't watch the van being loaded. We drove over to the coast so I wouldn't have to see it. Kathy assured me that the new owners seemed very nice.

That evening I packed some soup and cookies and went to meet Nancy and Jerry Fischman. My fears were greatly allayed as we chatted for a while. As time went by I discovered that they were people of many talents.

Next door on the other side, Dominic and Julie also decided to sell their house. The list price was $810,000. They were moving to Clear Lake after many years in Kenwood. They sold to Omar and Rosa Paz, a Mexican landscaper and his wife. This alarmed Don and Betty, who lived on the next property and they decided to sell, too. We were surprised because they had done extensive remodeling to the house. They had also added a large building to house their RV and provide room for an office. We often saw Don working outside and he seemed to thoroughly enjoy it. Don and Betty had planned to move closer to their daughter eventually, but decided to go right away. They were packed and gone in a month.

Nancy and Jerry made more improvements to the bed and breakfast. The house was brought up to the best that it could be. Nancy worked with a decorator as they chose colors and furniture. They decided that returning to the Arts and Crafts period, which was the style of the house, would be best. Muir Manor was renamed Birmingham Bed and Breakfast. Nancy said they liked England, and also they had had good luck and were happy when they lived in southern California on Birmingham Street.

Omar and Rosa were busy, too. The front yard became a showpiece with a dry creek, trees, flowers, fountain, and an impressive stone wall next to the road. They turned the garage and breezeway into living quarters. I wasn't sure how many people lived there.

Their backyard was interesting. One day we were outside behind our house with friends. Jean said, "Is that man leading a cow?" Yes, it was a cow and eventually there were four. We didn't complain but evidently somebody did and Rosa said they were allowed only one. Then we saw a goat and a lamb. Elizabeth McCoughy, a little girl who lived in the house behind us next door to Mirons, was delighted when a rabbit appeared occasionally in their yard. The goat wasn't a good idea. It ate too much of the bark before Omar put wire protection around the two redwood trees, which were about 80-feet tall. The trees died and had to be removed.

Rosa and Omar very much enjoyed birds. It seemed to be part of their culture. They had beautiful birds caged both outside and inside. Gradually the larger animals disappeared but a large flock of chickens remained. Somehow they managed to have more than one rooster, which puzzled me. Roosters of my experience tended to fight.

Rosa and Omar often entertained. They put in a swimming pool and a large trampoline. In August they had a fiesta and added a blow-up bouncy house for the children. Rosa warned me when that was going to happen because there was music and a microphone. They brought food to us and to Nancy and Jerry. Nancy said maybe that was to soothe us, but none of us really minded the party.

Occasionally we Kenwood girls got together. Nancy invited us for afternoon tea at her lovely home. They came to my house for my 77th birthday. Nancy and I invited the group to Doce Lunas, a fine Kenwood restaurant, to celebrate our March birthdays. Nancy's friend, Tammy Sakanashi, a Turtle Creek resident, joined us.

Judy Watten, Shirley Coops, Nancy Fischman,
Barb Davis May 2006

Kenwood was always changing in some way. Even more wineries were added. The local grocery was completely remodeled and some other small businesses opened. We plan to stay here as long as we're able.

01/01/00
A Summary of the Beginning Century

There was discussion about which year the next century really begins. Purists argued that it should be at the beginning of 2001. But it was natural to celebrate at the end of 1999 and beginning of 2000. This change had been anticipated with dread by anybody concerned with record-keeping, because they weren't sure how computers could handle it. The fear was that Y2K might destroy records and cause all sorts of other mischief. A lot of money was spent to combat possible complications. To pessimists' great surprise, there was little disruption. Life continued on as usual.

My 70th birthday arrived as expected. Other events of early 2000 were the long-anticipated opening of a bed and breakfast in Dad Coops' old house, and our eighth and last grandchild was born. I ventured into the Internet world, a wonderland with paths leading in all directions. Presidential debates between Al Gore and George Bush before the election of 2000 provided great material for the TV show, "Saturday Night Live." The suspense drama went on and on before Bush finally was the new president.

I had to write at least one letter on 01/01/01 because I wanted to use that date. That was one of the most orderly things about 2001. Being in "Rotating Outage Block 03" with periodic electric power loss was frustrating. This seemed to be a result of deregulating power generation and there was much finger-pointing.

A difficult situation was happening in our family, too. After 20 years of marriage Michael and Melinda were divorced. She said it felt as though a "huge load had been lifted," and she never had a moment of regret. I found that I had a problem, too, the discovery that I was a candidate for full-blown diabetes. A change of diet made my numbers normal, and also reduced my weight by 20 pounds.

But the worst happening of 2001 was on September 11, a beautiful day in New York City, when terrorists hijacked airliners and crashed them into the Twin Towers. The country watched in disbelief as our wonderful buildings collapsed into a heap of rubble, amidst which nearly 3000 people died. Things haven't been the same since. Our country has an obsession with having things 100% safe and now nothing seems safe.

We were directly touched on September 20 when we had plane reservations to fly to Pittsburgh. There was no curb side check-in, and we joined a line that stretched through the San Francisco airport. We were all dragging our luggage. Every time we've flown since then, another layer of security has been added. On one memorable departure my under-wire bra set off the buzzer. The latest precaution was a full-body scan. But we weren't deterred from taking many trips, from apple-tasting in Vermont to Christmas in Seattle, and points in between, as we visited friends and family.

We enjoyed an unusual happening in early 2002 when snow covered the ground in Kenwood. We walked through the neighborhood and there was a party atmosphere with snowmen, snowballs, smiles and laughter, and much picture-taking.

Art and Shirley Coops
50th Anniversary

Then came summer, and we drove to our 50th anniversary celebration in Estes Park, Colorado. Our wedding had been in May, but

169

this get-together was July 10-14, 2002. Family came from Pennsylvania, Washington, Vermont, Florida, and Michigan. It isn't easy to plan a reunion with such a far-flung family. After the celebration, I watched as people left for their various destinations. We started our drive home, and at the motel I had a meltdown because everybody was gone and I felt so sad.

Our anniversary in 2003 wasn't happy. I picked up the mail, which was unusual because Art almost always did that task. There was a letter to Art with an unfamiliar California return address. I said it was probably about the Cal Alumni Association. I wish he had lied and said, "Yes, that's what it was." But he didn't think it was a big deal, and told me it was from a woman he dated in college. He had gotten her address by writing to the alumni organization and had been corresponding with her for several years.

I was stunned. He explained that he thought my health was failing to the point that I would die, and he would be left alone. He thought this threatened his own life. He seemed to think I shouldn't be upset. Not so. It shook my belief that I could totally trust him more than anybody else in the whole world. I never felt quite the same again.

But as I thought about it, I concluded that Art's engineer's mind worked like that. He planned everything carefully and dispassionately. I'd lived with him for fifty-one years, and we had gone through a lot together. He was such a good daddy, a good provider, and had always given situations his thoughtful consideration. He didn't identify with romance, and I knew that. But still, it made me feel not very special. Was I so easily replaceable? I made it clear that I wouldn't stand for anything like that happening again.

The Iraq War started the next year. There isn't a direct connection, but we decided to update our will, create a trust, and reserve spots in the cemetery. All kinds of real estate was gaining in value as the decade continued. Several of our neighbors took advantage of this and decided to sell. Our children were moving, too, because of either job changes or family circumstances. Alison and family moved from Florida to Virginia, the Dan Clan from Vermont to Texas, Melinda had a new house in Pittsburgh, and Dinah and family moved to a bigger house in Seattle.

One of the moves that affected us the most was when Kathy and Ray Yahr sold the bed and breakfast in early 2005. I couldn't bear to watch as the moving van was loaded and the Yahrs and Kathy's parents, the

Mitchells, moved out. I was apprehensive about having different people there, but Nancy and Jerry Fischman are wonderful neighbors too. We also met Rosa and Omar Paz who moved in next door on the other side. I like them, and seeing the Mexican culture in action has been a new experience.

Economic times were good. Those who wanted jobs could find them. Investments and real estate all appeared to be doing fine. But now we know it was illusory. Forces had been building, and in 2008, to the amazement of even the experts, "sure things" weren't sure at all. The last few years of the decade were tumultuous. Nobody escaped the political, environmental, and economic upheavals. One of the biggest shocks was the abrupt drop in real estate values. Many people who took advantage of an opportunity for home ownership found themselves owing more money than their houses were worth. President Barack Obama took office just as these changes were taking place. He had promised "change" but it's unlikely this is what he had in mind.

FRIENDSHIP

Dick and Jane's dog isn't named Spot. She's a friendly black Lab whose name is Maggie. Maggie greeted us when we pulled into the driveway of the large western Pennsylvania farm. I had been looking forward to visiting and reminiscing with my old school friends, Dick and Jane. Besides seeing them again, both Art and I enjoyed catching a glimpse of farm life.

It was early May 2010. Planting was underway on the nearly 600 acres, plus several hundred rented acres where custom farming is done for neighbors. Sowing sometimes went on until 10:30 at night. Corn and soy beans are the principal crops. Dick watches the commodities market closely, and is still in the process of selling last year's harvest

One of Dick and Jane's sons now carries much of the work load on the farm. Besides the crops, there are beautiful Black Angus cattle on the farm. At one time, raising pigs was the main endeavor, so there's been an evolution of farming enterprises.

The large brick house was built about 1870. Dick and Jane have lived there for 51 years and have made many improvements and upgrades, besides the inevitable maintenance that an old house requires. The house is furnished with distinctive antiques, both inherited ones, and those found on Jane's antique shopping excursions.

Dick and Jane will both mark their 80th birthdays this year. Jane recognizes that fact and feels the need to cut back, but Dick charges on with enthusiasm and pride in their accomplishments, and eager for the next big project. There's activity all day long with trucks and equipment coming and going, sometimes making a rush trip to pick up a part for a broken machine. Maggie takes all this activity calmly and doesn't bark, except one day a red pickup truck came in the drive. Maggie ran after the truck and barked furiously. Jane said that somebody in that truck had once abused the dog, and she remembered.

At one time the farm had a large flock of chickens. Now there's only one big red hen left, and Jane says she has to be at least 14 years old.

Therein lies another tale of friendship, besides Jane's and mine. Often dogs enjoy chasing chickens, but Maggie, the dog, and Chook, the hen,

are companions who spend time together. They know each others needs, and Chook pecks from Maggie's food dish. They nap side by side.

Maggie watches every afternoon as Chook heads for the barn and soon comes out cackling. That's her proud announcement that she's laid an egg in her cozy nest in the hay. Maggie goes to the barn and has her snack, a delicious freshly-laid egg.

One day early last winter, Jane saw Maggie lying motionless in the flower bed and thought her dog was dead. But the dog stirred and appeared to be very sick, possibly with a fever. Jane helped her into the garage

Art Coops with Maggie & Chook

where she lay still and wouldn't eat or drink. Jane tried various tempting offerings of food and milk, but Maggie wasn't able to eat.

Apparently Chook knew something was wrong. The eggs in her nest were untouched. What was wrong with her friend? Was it instinct that made her lay an egg in the garage near Maggie? Jane then found a second egg there. The following day a third egg, and only the shells from the first two.

Soon Maggie was feeling better, was up and around, and was her good-natured self again. Did the hen save the dog's life? It would appear so.

◄◄ | ►►

FAMILY REUNION IN AUSTIN, TEXAS

With our family scattered all over the country, getting together is a major project. We managed to meet in Austin, Texas, over the week of July 26-August 1, 2006 when son, Dan, and his wife, Amy, hosted us at their home. They have a big house, but accepted the kindness of friendly neighbors who provided extra bedrooms.

One not-as-generous neighbor wouldn't be at home, and although the guests could use the bedrooms, they were not to use the A/C. That problem was solved only when Dan agreed to pay for the extra electricity.

Ages of reunion participants ranged from 6 to 80, with 2006 being a particularly significant year. Art turned 80, Melinda 50, Dan 40, Jonathan 20, and both Lauren and Tess, 10 years old. There was a big cake inscribed, "Happy 200 Years," although they did have to count the two 10-year-olds as only one so they could arrive at the magic number.

All eight grandchildren: Tess Havis, Andrew and Jessica Ludwig, Ryan and Brendan Coops, Pat and Jon (Jonathan) Spring, Lauren Ludwig
Austin July 2006

The wide age difference sometimes necessitated dividing into groups to accommodate different interests and abilities. One day some family members went to a tourist attraction called "The Cathedral of Junk." Since then, neighbors there have taken legal action because to them it was more "junk" than "cathedral," and they wanted to end the collecting and stop the invasion of fascinated tourists who were attracted by it.

The Cathedral was closed while the City Council pondered the question: who should they support, the "Make Austin Normal" group, or those who want to "Keep Austin Weird?" Tourists raved about experiencing a wonderland of memories, and the ingenious ways cast-offs were displayed, while safety experts feared somebody could be badly hurt. There was a frightful violation of city codes. Normal vs. Weird, a never-ending question.

Another activity was kayaking on Lady Bird Lake, while others went to Travis Lake where Amy took us out on a pontoon boat. We cruised for a while, and then she anchored in a cove where the youngsters had a great time swimming off the boat. Swimming was a daily activity because there's a nice pool at the house.

Everybody went to Lyndon Baines Johnson's Texas History Museum. Political power was in evidence by the huge multi-story structure and displays so extensive that they got boring. The children liked the I-MAX theater better.

Did I really want to go to see the World's Largest Urban Bat Colony? We set off with lawn chairs, blankets, and a cooler of refreshments, and ready for the nightly attraction. The bats' habitat is under a bridge in downtown Austin where Congress Avenue spans Town Lake, one of many lakes formed by dams on the Colorado River. Many other people had also made the decision to see this spectacle, so it took a while to park and then make our way to the viewing location.

It seemed to be a very strange way to spend an evening, but then we heard a murmur of excitement run through the crowd. "They're coming out!" Yes, they were, thousands of bats were emerging from under the bridge. They kept coming until they covered the sky like dark clouds. Estimates of the number range from 750,000 to 1.5 million bats. It's said that they devour up to 30,000 pounds of insects every night. In the winter all the bats leave and then return again in the spring. The female bats are pregnant.

On another day, five of our intrepid adventurers went canoeing under the bat bridge, turned around, and paddled under it in the other direction. They said, "Nothing like getting another whiff of a million bats."

I mentioned the cooler loaded with refreshments that was carried to the bat viewing. Eating and drinking were major activities every day and everywhere. One evening Art and I hosted the family at the Oasis, a good restaurant, with a view. Dan and Amy had prepared mountains of food for meals at their house. I was also impressed by the mountain of trash that we produced.

Pile Up on Patrick with Andrew,
Brendan, Ryan, Tess, Lauren, & Jessica

Eight grandchildren who were ages 6-20 provided endless attraction for me as I thought things like, "He looks so much like his mom," or "They're all computer nerds," or "She has gorgeous long legs."

The older grandchildren were indulgent of the younger ones. One evening when the kids piled on top of Jon and Pat as they sat on the sofa, they all enjoyed it. It was good for the cousins to get better acquainted.

Some family members had to go home, but those of us still there had one last adventure. We toured the natural Inner Space Cavern, an impressive underground experience. The formations were magnificent.

The Family

The next day everybody had to leave to go back to their homes and jobs. Dan took us to the airport where we got aboard a United plane for the direct flight to San Francisco. It had been a dream trip, one where we got to enjoy our growing family.

IN MEMORIAM:

ARTHUR IRVING COOPS 1926-2011

O n February 12, 2011, Art suffered a massive thalamus hemorrhage. The following are messages I sent by e-mail and blog to friends and family:

Sunday, February 13, 2011 10:00 AM

Art had a stroke last night, and is in ICU at Memorial Hospital in Santa Rosa. I don't know yet how bad it is. It's a "thalamus hemorrhage" in the right side of his brain, so the left side of his body is affected. Our neighbors were wonderful. Nancy took me to the hospital and stayed with me until Art was settled in the ICU. His speech is slurred, but he knows what he's talking about. It was all so sudden, one minute fine and then...

Monday, February 14, 2011 5:22 PM

I know I'll have a meltdown somewhere along the way, but it's really nice now with both Dan and Dinah here. None of us can believe that Art is in this predicament. The blood in the brain isn't large, but enough to paralyze the left side of his body. The muscles are strong as ever, but not getting signals.

Dan and Dinah are at their computers looking up info about the whole situation. We're to have a consultation tomorrow about possible outcomes, but we know those vary widely. The speech therapist gave Art a swallowing test today and he didn't pass yet, but may be able to in a couple of days. Meanwhile he has a feeding tube. My thoughts are on overload. What next? Even experts can only give typical scenarios.

Wednesday, February 16, 2011 6:35 AM

Things are crazy-weird here with Art's sudden attack. I'm so glad both Dinah and Dan can be with us now, not thinking too well. The kids have been wonderful.

A message just came from Dan at the hospital that the new CT is done. Art didn't have a good night. They don't let him sleep long at a time—keep checking for stuff. He's terribly fatigued, which comes with a stroke anyway. We just have to wait and see. We're so impressed with the hospital staff. Dinah said it's the best she's ever seen.

This stroke was devastating. We're all wondering if it would have been better if it had been immediately fatal, because this week has been awful for all of us, including him. He never lost consciousness and has been aware of what's happening. His speech is slurred and often hard to understand. Today has been very busy with making the many arrangements.

Friday, February 18, 2011 6:03 PM

I'm at the hospital and writing on Dinah's computer. Melinda, Dinah, and Dan are here and Alison is on the airporter headed to Santa Rosa. Art will come home tomorrow in an ambulance and will be under hospice care. It took hours of intense discussion and making arrangements to allow this to happen. The doctors and hospital are following Art's Advance Health Care Directive (I'm so glad we had those drawn up) for extraordinary care, or not, and the wishes of the family.

Dinah, Dan, and Alison

179

It is great to have Art home, even though this is a difficult and sorrowful time, and I had to arrange for around-the-clock caretakers. But this worked best for our family. It's nice that he is here where we can be with him anytime without many long trips for a few minutes in a care home.

February 20-26, 2011

Art is in the bed here beside me in the room. He's terribly bored. He isn't in the habit of staying put, and the outdoors is calling. He's sure he could walk if we would help him out of bed. In fact, he says he DID walk. This is very hard to comprehend for all of us. We often have to strain to catch his words and answer questions.

We had one wonderful evening. The kids set up a slide show of pictures from the 1960s and 1970s. Art had his glasses on, sat up, was able to focus, and enjoyed remembering many happy family happenings. He looked and acted like himself. It made it seem as though there was hope, but those were the only really hopeful moments in the week.

There were some sorrowful times too, but it was good he was in familiar surroundings. He can only eat small amounts of pureed food because the stroke destroyed his ability to swallow, and food and even saliva are aspirated into his lungs. This week certainly isn't like anything I've ever experienced before.

Sunday, February 27, 2011 10:40 AM

I was in another room, and Daria the care-giver was helping with cleaning the house. Dinah called us because she noticed a different color in Art's face. We stood beside him, and his breaths came further and further apart. I said, "He did just breathe again, didn't he?" She shook her head "no" and wrote 9:45 in her record book. I kept talking to him, because I'd read somewhere that a person can still hear for a little while.

The hospice nurse arrived, checked Art, and she, too, shook her head "no" and wrote in her record book. I wasn't sure what to do, but the hospice nurse and care-giver did.

We didn't ask that he be taken away immediately, because Melinda and Jonathan were arriving in the afternoon. When Melinda and grandson Jonathan arrived, Melinda said when they were almost here, she suddenly started sobbing, even though she didn't know Art had died.

We just heard that Alison came through her surgery well, but she won't be able to fly here again for the service. Jonathan can't be here either. He needs to leave in a couple of days, but Melinda can stay. Many people need to arrange air travel, so we finalized plans for the memorial, which will be March 10 at 11:00 am at the Sonoma United Methodist Church.

COOPS, Arthur Irving

Arthur Irving Coops was born in Sonoma on May 31, 1926, the son of Arthur A. Coops and Aloha Millard Coops. On February 12, 2011 at age 84 he suffered a thalamus hemorrhage and died on February 27 at home under hospice care. His only complaint was "I'm so bored." On most days before the stroke he had been outside with his planting, pruning, trimming, mowing, and harvesting. It was an enjoyable retirement after 43 years as an electrical engineer at Westinghouse Electric's Transformer Division in Sharon, Pennsylvania. Art received his education at Sonoma Valley schools and was a 1944 graduate of Sonoma Valley High School. From there he went to the University of California at Berkeley in the Navy V-12 program and graduated in 1948. He is survived by Shirley Shannon Coops, his wife of 58 years, four children, eight grandchildren, and a brother, Melvin Coops, Oakmont. Daughters are: Melinda Coops Spring, Pittsburgh, Pennsylvania, Dinah Coops Havas (Steve), Seattle, Washington, and Alison Coops Ludwig (Charles), Richmond, Virginia. Son Daniel Coops (Amy), lives in Austin, Texas. Grandchildren are Jonathan and Patrick Spring, Jessica, Andrew, and Lauren Ludwig, Tess Havas, and Ryan and Brendan Coops. Friends and family are invited to a memorial service on Thursday, March 10, at 11:00 AM at the Sonoma United Methodist Church, 109 Patten St., Sonoma, California. Art very much enjoyed flowers, but donations to the church or to Memorial Hospice would also be welcome. DUGGAN'S MISSION CHAPEL

I realized yesterday that I hadn't included Betty's name in anything. I should have said "preceded in death by his sister, Betty Coops James." She was a lovely lady and we liked her very much. I feel awful about it.

Last night I kept dreaming about trying to figure out a new cell phone, trying to click the right place on my computer—lots of keys and attempted clicking. I'd wake up every couple of hours, and then go back to work on gadgets while asleep. If I were 20 (or more) years younger I'd be having a great time with this stuff. As Art kept saying after the stroke, "I'm trying to figure this out."

Next door, Omar's been having a rough time, too, with family bereavements. He said he would help get a neighbor to sing the Spanish parts of a hymn at Art's service. Omar also agreed to set a trap for a critter that apparently is living in the garage.

Sunday, March 6, 2011 9:44 PM

Melinda and I went to church. It was good to see folks. I certainly felt surrounded by love and caring. I was also glad to get some of the "first time I've seen you since..." over with.

I think my friend Maxine had the right interpretation of my technology dream. She thinks it was about facing life without my life partner. She went through this ordeal a few years ago. I'd already thought of what she said about people helping me. They are God's angels sent to help and care for me.

Tomorrow a.m. our attorney is scheduled to call, and in the PM we're to go to the cemetery for the inurnment of the ashes. Pastor Pam Cummings said she would be there with Melinda and me. One unbelievable day after another.

Tuesday, March 8, 2011 3:28 PM

There will never be another day like this. I say that every day now. We went to Sonoma and the cemetery. An attendant opened the crypt. He left for a while, and Pam shared beautiful scripture, poems, sayings, and prayers. When we called him back, he was carrying a hand-full of beautiful daffodils. We thought he was going to give each of us a flower, but he put them in with the box of ashes.

Safeway next to order the food for Thursday. Bill Morris said he would pick it up; that will help. Melinda bought a big posterboard for mounting pictures for the memory table. Omar's friend and our neighbor, Carlos Herrera, will sing and play the guitar at the Thurs. service.

Melinda and I talked about Art's big farm tractor. I guess we'll have to see about some discing. I know Art was particular about the soil being to the proper dryness. One more thing I know nothing about.

Haircut tomorrow. That sounds so normal, hope it will be. Nancy's cleaning person came today, and she's a real pro. I'm thrilled with what she was able to do on jobs that I knew were there, undone. Dan and Dinah are scheduled to arrive tomorrow. I'm afraid that when I have a spare minute, I'll start to think about everything.

Thursday, March 10, 2011 8:27 PM

We appreciated having friends at Art's memorial service. Everyone was so supportive; it was good to hear the lovely comments about Art. Our church friends are wonderful; Pastor Pam Cummings, Darlene, Rich, Loretta, etc. We enjoyed the music a lot. The flowers are gorgeous; we have them at home now. Melinda takes over as the family's Master Gardener; she keeps an eye on the growing things. We've found excellent help for when just I am here, because plant life will be in jeopardy then.

After the Memorial Service:
Dinah and Shirley

Flowers from
Dorothy,
Michael, etc.
Families

Melinda

183

Another day that seemed impossible. We've been hearing about the earthquake-tsunami in Japan. Meanwhile, it was a very nice sunny day here. We would love to have Alison with us, too. Four kids together are even better than three. We laugh amidst the sadness. They thought I needed a GPS since I'll be driving alone, so we got one at Best Buy.

The flock of sheep is still weeding the vineyard up the road, very picturesque. At home, Dinah and Melinda went for a walk while Dan talked to neighbor Omar. It's drastic, but there's a consensus that we need a dumpster to clean out the shed and behind it. Nancy was here, too. We'll try to save things that are worthwhile.

So it goes, one busy day after another. The kids said they were getting sore from the worn out dining room chairs. We found a quaint little upholstery shop run by a delightful old couple. No decision yet.

Omar supplied a trap to set in the garage. Something hissed at Melinda when she was out there last evening. All the kids agree there's a critter there, at least at night.

In today's mail, there were more thoughtful remembrances, very much appreciated. Happy Birthday to my brother today. My birthday is Sunday, not so happy.

Saturday, March 12, 2011 9:22 PM

The kids did a great job sorting things in the shed into trash, possible sale, and keepers. But the accumulation is only diminished and lots still there. The kids will all be leaving soon, but planning to come back and do more, probably including a yard sale.

I heard an engine running for a long time, and discovered Omar's daughter mowing our grass. She's 15, and seems to be having a good time. It's really very nice of the family.

We think our garage critter is a cat. We often see neighborhood cats exploring, and sometimes turning on the automatic garage light if the door is open. Cats are better than rats.

The tractor started after a battery charge. Daniel looked

Melinda, Dan, and Dinah

as delighted as when he was little and started a lawn tractor in a store display. The kids finished sorting 1,200 color slides, choosing 800 to put on DVD.

The house has been full of laughter and reminisces. Dan goes home tomorrow to his family and job. The girls leave Monday and Tuesday. They'll come again, plus grandchildren. It was four weeks ago this evening that the horrible stroke hit. What a month, incomprehensible.

Sunday, Monday, March 13-14, 2011 8:34 PM

It's one impossible day after another. Dan went home yesterday, and this p.m. Dinah flew back to Seattle. A (saintly) neighbor and I will take Melinda to the airporter bus in Santa Rosa EARLY tomorrow a.m.

Melinda, Shirley, and Dinah

for her all-day trip back to Pittsburgh. The kids are excited to be going home. It was wonderful to have them here, and there's not much else they can do right now. We can all think about it for a while, and decide what to try to plan for next. Lots of rain on my birthday yesterday. Then, in the evening, thunder and lightning, very rare indeed. I'd believe almost anything.

Tuesday, March 15, 2011 8:11 PM

Barb, one of my great neighbors, drove Melinda and me to the airporter bus in Santa Rosa. Many people were also waiting, so it didn't seem so weird to be somewhere before 5 a.m. I'm so glad she drove because I hardly ever drive in the dark. It was raining, too.

So here I am alone. I'm still so astonished that I'm the one who's left. We both assumed that Art would live much longer. He would be having quite different problems than I do, mostly about fixing food, while the outside stuff scares me. I have good folks to help me with that, so I'd better stay put for a while. But I'll still look around at senior complexes to see what might work for me. Deciding what to fit into half the space I have now won't be easy.

I'm getting papers together to take to the meeting with the attorney next week. All the lawyer has told me so far is not to sign things, or buy or sell anything until we talk. I'll go along with that. I did talk to the VA and to Social Security, or to their machines.

Pastor Pam Cummings was a wonderful help through all this; it would have been so much harder without her. I think we totally confused her with all the different branches of the family who have lived so many different places. I'd better clear it up that Art grew up on a ranch on the Napa Road outside Sonoma. His family lost that place in 1938 when he was 12, and then they lived in Sonoma. Art's dad didn't buy the Kenwood property until 1956, and Art had been living in Pennsylvania for 8 years by then.

Wednesday, March 16, 2011 9:50 PM

I think it's good advice to not make any big decisions for at least a year. Tomorrow is my appointment in Sonoma at the Hearing Center. Getting used to hearing aids has been an easy part of the last month.

St. Pat's Day, Thursday, March 17, 2011 9:23 PM

I have my notepaper ready to start expressing my gratitude for the many kindnesses. I'm glad I didn't say "in lieu of flowers" because I'm still enjoying their beauty. Art did enjoy growing flowers and thought they should stay out there where they belonged! My life is going off in an entirely different direction, and nothing is the same. This is all me now, a scary thought indeed.

Scoops Blog

Tuesday, March 29, 2011

A blog? Really? One of my granddaughters is working on donations for the Relay for Life at her college. She supports many good causes. I asked her if there's an organization for "Tech-Challenged Grandmas."

It's been a month since Art's death. The hospice chaplain came today. She said it's probably good to try to keep busy. Try? There are way too many things to do, and I'm adding to that by doing extra cleaning projects, don't know why.

The broker called this p.m.; there are decisions to be made about investments. I'm to see the attorney again on Thursday.

This evening was good. I had dinner with Nancy and Jerry from the bed and breakfast.

Thursday, March 31, 2011

My phone and internet were out yesterday p.m. and evening. They're back, so is this normal, or are things normal without them? Doesn't matter, nothing is normal for me anyway. Today I had another intense hour with the attorney, and then went to get my teeth cleaned, quite a fun morning.

I visited with Barb, who invited me to go to a seminar with her about women who are alone and must make decisions about investments. When I was leaving her house, she walked out to the street with me, and we both felt as though Art would come walking up the street any minute. Sometimes, when I used to stop and talk, Art would keep on walking, and I'd still be standing there chatting when he came back.

My favorite radio station seems to be taking a turn to the left. The other night a guy was talking about religion, and how ignorant it all is. He was filling in for somebody, hope he goes away. Faith, and the people of faith certainly have helped me through this tragedy. The Bible is ancient, but still wise and comforting.

Friday, April 1, 2011

April Fool! I wonder if I should have tried texting, tweeting, or Facebook? Isn't there a limit of 140 characters? That would have shut me up. This way, nothing will. Except when my internet and phone are out, which happened again today.

"Keeping busy" is good, but I'd rather not be this busy. I had errands at seven different places today. And deciphering the paperwork can be difficult. I'm trying to keep topics sorted and in their own piles.

Art would have been outside most of the time on these nice days. I'm not sure what projects he would have worked on. He would have been enjoying his many springtime activities. All I'm going to do is try to keep our house from disappearing in vegetation.

Saturday, April 2, 2011

It's another lovely day, and I did walk some. I tend to do more talking than walking. Todd and Mary live on the property adjoining ours, and I stopped in to visit. Mary and son Harrison showed me the four adorable new baby chicks that they bought a couple of days ago, so that will bring the flock to 15. Mary said she can come to Nancy's and my birthday luncheon Saturday. Lots of nice Kenwood girlfriends!

Dan called today. He's helping keep track of the investment scene. I'm still in the process of getting my name alone put on the trust and IRA, and that means lots of paper-signing. We won't worry about any buying and selling or moving things around until everything is properly titled. We'll think about where to go from there. No hasty decisions. We are thinking about a get-together in mid-July. .

Sunday, April 3, 2011

There are so many changes going on at the same time. It's a different world without Art here. Then there's the technology. I know I'm slower, but aren't tech changes coming faster than they used to? And no mistakes are tolerated. I may have sent the wrong blog address to dozens of people because I left out a period. Here's the right one: http://www. scoops1952.blogspot.com, with a period after 1952.

There are many good friends at church, but going there this morning was difficult because Art and I always went together, and Art often helped with ushering. I went to the early service today; always like to see the children and younger folks who go then.

I'll have to manage investments, but will depend on people more knowledgeable. I also need a new cell phone, but can't face that challenge right now.

The weather was pleasant. In the p.m., I walked to the Kenwood soccer park, sat on a bench, and called my sister for a chat. I looked at the beautiful mountains and people romping with their dogs. It was a peaceful scene, but this time, Art didn't come up the path after his longer walk.

Monday, April 4, 2011

It was so nice on the back deck that I didn't come in until the sun went down, and I even ate out there. But it's teaser weather, and is to be cool and damp later in the week. Some plants looked thirsty so I gave them a drink. I feel sorry for all the growing things around here. I'll do the best I can.

The church used-book sale was a big success. I started reading one of the books I bought, "Tuesdays with Morrie." I read it a long time ago, and forgot that Morrie was suffering from ALS. A neighbor was afflicted with that, so it means more to me now. Also, I just lost somebody precious.

One of the jobs Art had taken on was to mow a path across the empty lot on the way to the P.O. Today it was mowed, and a neighbor said he had done it. I was so pleased.

Tuesday, April 5, 2011

I decided to take the info I'd collected to the attorney, so went to Sonoma this morning. I think I can finish settling Art's estate myself, with the children's help. Art and I didn't raise dummies. The remaining documentation, etc., looks straightforward, so I'll work on it.

Since I was in town I decided to have lunch there. My fortune cookie said, "Now is a good time for you to explore. Take a vacation." The only exploring I'm doing is trying to navigate life as a widow. I hate that word. Friends and family are helping me adjust.

Saturday, April 9, 2011

Nancy and I finally had our March birthday party. Eight Kenwood girlfriends met for lunch at Doce Lunas, a local restaurant. Nancy brought champagne, and we had a good celebration. When we finally get together, we always wonder why we don't do it more often, but everybody is busy and there's only so much time and energy.

As the weather gets nicer and drier, I miss Art more and more. Everywhere I look I see things that he would be working on this time of year, and it's very strange to be here by myself. We'll have some sort of garden. Bill plans to plant a few things, and Nancy and Jerry will, too. Nancy thinks we should have some zucchini. Oh, yes, zucchini. I suppose even I could grow that.

Today's e-mail from my brother says they could come to visit June 30-July 7. Alison's visit is scheduled for May 17-23, and a couple of the other kids hope to be here mid-July. I think there will be plenty to do. My new checks came with only my name. I haven't been able to open them yet. It's so unbelievable. I see there are more proxies, too. What a strange new world.

Sunday, April 10, 2011

Sunday mornings are different than other mornings. Today my morning was quiet and lonely. It was good to take a walk in the evening.

I saw Nancy, and then walked to Judy's house. There was a wonderful aroma of fresh-baked bread as I approached. We had a nice chat, and she made some prints of a picture from yesterday's birthday lunch. She walked up to the corner with me.

At the corner, there was a car with people who seemed to be waiting for me. It was Kathy and Ray Yahr, so I got to talk to them, and also give Kathy a print of the picture from the luncheon. When I got home, Nancy and Jerry were sitting outside, and we talked about the garden, watering, the high grass around the garden, and the tractor.

Art would never have let things look like this. The lawn guy is to come on Tuesday, and I hope there will be big improvements. I'm also going to get help with cleaning inside the house. Bill said he plans to come both Monday and Tuesday to work on the barn clean-out. He says he has a mandate from the kids, and he's rising to the challenge.

Tuesday, April 12, 2011

At one point today, there were three trucks here. Trino and his helper worked on lawn care, Bill came to load his truck with Habitat for Humanity possibilities, and his contractor friend came to look over the wood supply. It's obvious stepbrother Bill has been a tremendous help through all this. I don't want him to overdo, and I think he's done enough, but he said he's coming again on Thursday. I may have to say "no more."

Trino plans to come again tomorrow and start the watering system. He and his helper did a great job today. I think the berries will suffer Art's loss, too. He gave them hours of care, which I couldn't do even if I wanted to. It seems for each thing I cross off my to-do list, I have to add two more.

Wednesday, April 13, 2011

I googled "shrew," as that might be what's living in the garage. Shrews aren't rodents, but related to moles. I've caught glimpses of the critter a couple of times. It doesn't move as fast as mice and rats. I'll think of it as my pet until I can figure out what to do.

Meanwhile, Trino and his helper did a lot of work on the watering system. He said he could finish in another day. I'm sure some of Art's plants are getting thirsty. Timers will be more dependable about watering than I would or could be. This is a strange new life, and I feel like a different person doing different things.

Trino and his helper put in all kinds of water stuff today, so tomorrow at 7 a.m. things are supposed to start being watered. Trino also hung my hummingbird feeder, and I already saw a bird. Bill took another trailerfull from the barn-shed to the dump. It seems endless. There was a letter from the attorney in the mail, and I was almost afraid to open it, thinking it was another bill, but it just said he had been notified that I didn't owe the state of California any money. I'd heard that people who used Medi-Cal are asked to pay it back, so I'm sure those folks have received very nasty news in that kind of letter.

Barb and I went to the investment seminar today, but the presentation was disappointing. It was geared to much younger people who were being encouraged to save money with IRAs, etc. Many of us were past those opportunities, and are taking Required Minimum Distributions now.

I needed to go for a walk when I got home. I saw another neighbor who hadn't heard about Art and was stunned by the news. Folks always ask how they can help, and tell me I shouldn't hesitate to ask. We agreed that friends and family are all-important.

Friday, April 15, 2011

Checking out groceries today, I found I'd left my wallet at home! But they accepted the check. Other than that, the day was routine.

The water did indeed come on at 7 a.m., which must have been a huge relief to the plants. That project is nearly finished.

I saw neighbor Judy at the P.O. She was throwing away unwanted mail, but all of mine was important today. There's another paper to sign, requests for a death certificate, and proof that I'm who I say I am. There's also a request for a document that I'm not sure what they mean. I'll have to call. Judy said that the Life Story writing classes have been cancelled due to a cut-off of state funds for Santa Rosa Junior College. I hope the class can continue somehow. It was a big help to me, speaking of which, if I'm to get my book printed this year I'd better get back to it.

Saturday, April 16, 2011

It looked like a boring day with nobody to talk to, but Omar and his marvelous machine came. That annoying pile of old fill-dirt in the back field was leveled in less than five minutes. I talked to him about discing, and about hauling stuff away. I think getting rid of junk can be done before the kids come to work on Craig-listing and a yard sale.

Saturday evenings are hard. As 7:30 approaches, I re-live Art's awful stroke. The next few weekends were very bad, too. But people have been so great, and at times I enjoy the challenge of making decisions, and hope I don't make serious mistakes.

Palm Sunday, April 17, 2011

I went to early church today. After church I went to Friedman's, the big local hardware store. I rolled a cart through the nursery, but decided I'd better leave all the plants where they were so they would get dependable care. Instead, I looked for a toilet in the plumbing department. Art had tried to fix our "lemon," but it never worked right. I spent time in the evening looking around and writing down everything that I would ask Omar to haul away.

Monday, April 18, 2011

Our little token lawn has sprinklers now. Trino and his helper worked most of the day on completing the project. The plumber came and installed the new toilet. I mentioned that it takes a long time to get hot water to the kitchen. He checked the water heater and said, "Did you know your water heater is leaking?" He's installing a new water heater tomorrow.

I complied with another request to send a death certificate and proof that I'm who I claim to be.

Tuesday, April 19, 2011

I'm on a steep learning curve. The P.O. box was full, and the mail included a letter asking for more document copies. I'll work on that tomorrow. A fun thing was getting out a porch chair and sitting outside to read the paper, although reading the news wasn't at all soothing.

Thursday, April 21, 2011

Since I had to go to Santa Rosa for my doctor check-up, I also went to the upholstery shop with the chair seats, intending to pick one of the fabrics that we liked. Unfortunately, the books from which we had chosen had been borrowed by another customer. The nice lady said she would either get the books back, or request samples from the manufacturer. It was a bit scary to leave my seats there, because it seemed every available inch was already taken. It made me wonder if I'll ever see them again. But the folks seem to keep track of things, and I think eventually the chairs will be very pretty.

The GPS was a big help in finding the shop. It was soon time to tell the GPS "Go Home," but she didn't like the way I was going so I unplugged it. I didn't know I could do all this stuff.

Saturday, April 23, 2011

The sky is overcast, but it isn't cold. I actually worked outside a little. There's a big geranium among the rose bushes behind the garage, and I cut the dead stuff out of it. The roses are starting to bloom. I feel so sorry for the optimistically growing plants around here, but I'll do what I can for them.

I saw my little garage pet a couple of times today. He (or she) was scurrying across the driveway and into the garage. I blocked off a little space at one end of the garage door, and then felt bad that I wasn't letting him go back and forth to his home. Obviously I'm hard up for companionship around here. It will be good to go to church tomorrow, and then go to Oakmont for dinner with friends.

Easter Sunday and Monday, April 24 and 25, 2011

Flowers, music, and the service at church were lovely. The children's egg hunt didn't go well, because the weather was windy and drizzly. But it was sunny for going to dinner at writing-friend Millie's house. I was pleased to be included with her family. It was fun to meet folks I had heard about in her stories. The food and company were great.

DREAMS
APRIL 26, 2011

Nightmares aren't often a problem for me, and I'm not sure this one was a nightmare. I was impressed with how my brain condensed the last three months of grief, shock, unreality, frustration, and uncertainty into dream episodes that exactly expressed my experiences and feelings, and all in a short period of time.

I woke up, and it wasn't yet midnight. I lay there feeling exhausted from what I'd just been through. I got up and made some notes about what had happened.

One dream segment showed my discomfort with the language barrier. Not understanding, or being understood well by much of the community is a problem. I rang the bell at a Latino house, but they wouldn't answer, and I couldn't explain what I needed.

Next, the barn-shed: Nancy's grandson and a mischievous friend had climbed up onto the roof of Dad Coops' office that is in one corner of the barn. They wouldn't come down, and I said I would count to three and then go tell the boy's mother. I counted slowly, with no results, so went over to Nancy's. She and the other lady were just leaving and I could see them through the heavy glass. I tried tapping on the glass to get their attention, but the sound didn't get to them.

For some reason I was inside and they were walking away down the sidewalk. But I got to a door and told them about the little boys. We went out to the dark barn, and I found a light switch. The barn floor was covered with scraps of wood, even worse than it really is.

The scene shifted to a Kenwood street. I thought I was going into the Kenwood Press office, but these folks were scary. I briefly looked at their computer screen, but decided to leave, and I thought a big guy with a badly scarred face was going to follow me, but he didn't. I wanted to be home and be safe. I wasn't far from home, but walking was difficult. Usually in dreams I walk so easily I don't even notice it, but this time my body felt very heavy and exhausted. I decided I'd been trying to do too much.

I'm not sure it was at home, but I was in bed somewhere, and I thought my sister was in that house, too, and that would be good. I called, "Dorothy," but no answer. Then suddenly I was talking to her on the phone. She said our brother was at her house, too, as well as her L.A. son. She had many people in her house.

I stopped talking with her, but right away there was somebody else on the phone, and I couldn't hear or understand what they were saying. The dream felt like a perfect summary of recent experiences, exaggerated to be sure, but also quite accurate in recording what's been happening, and my reactions.

Made in the USA
San Bernardino, CA
13 December 2012